'Donald Trump and I both took economics degrees in the 1960s. This book describes the history which I learnt and Donald Trump has forgotten – or never understood. Philip Coggan's masterly exposition is easy to understand and (almost) impossible to forget' John Kay, author of *The Corporation in the Twenty-First Century* and *Obliquity*

'This book is a tour de force. The arguments are very clearly and succinctly put in a way that should convince anyone of the madness of the tariff policy' David Miles, professor of financial economics, Imperial College Business School

Philip Coggan is a former *Economist* and *Financial Times* journalist. In 2009, he was voted Senior Financial Journalist of the Year in the Wincott Awards and best communicator in the Business Journalist of the Year Awards. Among his books are *The Money Machine*, *Paper Promises*, the highly acclaimed *More: The 10,000-Year Rise of the World Economy* and *Surviving the Daily Grind*.

THE ECONOMIC CONSEQUENCES OF MR TRUMP

What the Trade War Means for the World

PHILIP COGGAN

Profile Books

First published in Great Britain in 2025 by
Profile Books Ltd
29 Cloth Fair
London
ECIA 7JQ
www.profilebooks.com

1 3 5 7 9 10 8 6 4 2

Typeset in Dante by MacGuru Ltd
Printed and bound in India by
Manipal Technologies Limited

A CIP catalogue record for this book is available from the British Library.

Our product safety representative in the EU is Authorised
Rep Compliance Ltd., Ground Floor, 71 Lower Baggot Street,
Dublin, D02 P593, Ireland. www.arccompliance.com

ISBN 978 1 80522 768 7
eISBN 978 1 80522 770 0

MIX
Paper | Supporting
responsible forestry
FSC™ C043100

CONTENTS

PREFACE

This book was written at speed because I was both amazed at Mr Trump's tariff announcement on 2 April, and energised into action because the grounds for criticism were so wide. Nevertheless, there were two daunting aspects. First, I do not have the intellect or the qualifications of John Maynard Keynes, whose book *The Economic Consequences of Mr Churchill* was my inspiration. Second, writing a book on the erratic and illogical policy of a temperamental president was always a hostage to fortune, as it proved until the last day. I persevered because the historical parallels are so striking and the case against the Trump tax needs to be stated. The chaos of the regime's policy changes is a key part of the argument; this is no way to run the world's largest economy.

Clare Grist Taylor and the team at Profile Books deserve enormous credit for recognising the merits of the idea and for acting so swiftly to bring it to fruition. I am grateful for wise advice from David Miles and Andy Haldane. And the wonderful Patrick Lane of the *Economist* read through the book to weed out errors and solecisms; Patrick is the epitome of the professional journalist and a class act.

Finally, love and thanks go to my wife, Sandra Kanthal, who proved a hugely useful font of ideas and also a reader who was not afraid to pull me up for using economic jargon. This book would not have existed without her.

As the subject of this book would say, thank you for your attention in this matter.

Philip Coggan
31 May 2025

INTRODUCTION

'Over the past 200 years, not only has the argument against tariffs and trade barriers won nearly universal agreement among economists but it has also proven itself in the real world, where we have seen free-trading nations prosper while protectionist countries fall behind.'

President Ronald Reagan, radio broadcast, 1988

'I always say tariff is the most beautiful word to me in the dictionary.'

President Donald Trump, January 2025

'For every complex problem there is an answer that is clear, simple and wrong.'

H. L. Mencken, satirist (1880–1956)

On 2 April 2025, President Donald Trump unveiled a package of tariffs on products from almost every nation in the world. The scale of these tariffs (which are taxes on imports) surprised observers around the globe and quickly sent financial markets into a tailspin. While Mr Trump said the announcement represented 'Liberation Day', the *Economist* quickly dubbed it 'Ruination Day'.

Exactly 100 years previously, in 1925, Winston Churchill, as chancellor of the exchequer, took Britain back onto the gold standard. John Maynard Keynes, the great economist, advised against the decision and published a book lambasting the move called *The Economic Consequences of Mr Churchill*. This book is a homage to Keynes's polemic and will argue that Mr Trump's package, and the confusing announcements that followed it, was one of the greatest economic policy mistakes in history.

The tariffs, or Trump tax, are a mistake in many different ways. But the most important error is a fundamental misunderstanding of the global trading system. The US does not make wholly American goods, nor the UK wholly British goods. Products are constructed from materials and components brought in from all over the world. Around half of all US cars are made from imported parts, for example.[1] When you impose tariffs on imported components, you increase the costs of domestic producers.

Furthermore, while Mr Trump keeps insisting that tariffs are paid by foreign countries, they are initially paid by the importing company; as revealed by the president's demand that Walmart, along with China, 'eat the tariffs' when the retailer said it would be forced to raise prices to reflect its increased costs.[2]

While Mr Trump seemed not to be aware of these issues, business groups and the financial markets definitely were. In the week following the 2 April announcement, there was financial turmoil, with share prices, bond prices and the dollar all falling. So, on 9 April, Mr Trump suspended for ninety days the higher tariff rates he had imposed on much of the world, cutting them back to a base level of 10 per cent.

The exceptions were Canada, Mexico and China. For the latter, after a surreal bout of tit-for-tat retaliation, the US raised tariffs to a prohibitive 145 per cent. But then, after a drop in deliveries at US ports and warnings from retailers about empty shelves, there was another retreat. On 12 May, both the US and China suspended the retaliatory measures for ninety days, leaving the US level at a still high, but not completely prohibitive, 30 per cent. Like the grand old duke of (New) York, Mr Trump had marched his tariffs to the top of the hill, and then marched them (mostly) back down again.

The markets reacted with relief, regaining all the losses suffered in early April. The hope was that Mr Trump had learned his lesson in the face of harsh reality. Nevertheless, the effective tariff rate on imports was much higher than before Mr Trump came to office. And, far from being discouraged from using the tariff weapon, the president seemed happy to wield it again. In mid-May he implied that he would levy differential tariffs on other nations within weeks, a breach of the previously announced ninety-day suspension and another bewildering change of tactic. And then on 23 May, he threatened to impose 50 per cent tariffs on imports from the European Union, only to withdraw that threat two days later.

At the end of May, the Court of International Trade in the US ruled that Mr Trump has exceeded his authority by imposing tariffs when the power should belong to Congress. Mr Trump had cited a 'national emergency' to justify his actions but there was no emergency; the US economy grew rapidly in 2024, unemployment was low and inflation was falling. While the ruling was good news, the world still could not rest easy. The Supreme Court might well overturn the decision and the president might find other ways to push the tariffs through. But the ruling emphasised the one consistent theme behind all the president's actions: chaos.

It is hard for readers (and authors) to keep up with this blizzard of announcements. To avoid confusion it is best to keep one thought in mind; by imposing tariffs, Mr Trump has made the goods Americans buy more expensive, and disrupted the global economy, without doing anything to help those who voted for him.

The hundred-year echo

The decisions of Winston Churchill and President Trump have some striking parallels. Keynes lamented that the consequences of a return to the gold standard would be a decline in the standard of living in the form of lower wages. Economists today worry that US workers will face a reduced standard of living in the form of higher prices.

Nostalgia also links the two proposals. Churchill was trying to recreate the conditions that existed before the First World War when Britain was the centrepiece of the global financial system, sterling was the pre-eminent currency and British industries were matched only by those of Germany and the US. Mr Trump is trying to recreate the conditions of the 1950s and 1960s, when US industry dominated the world and the men (and they were mostly men) employed in manufacturing could afford a house, a gas-guzzling car and all the latest gadgets.

Churchill's strategy was a mistaken reading of history. The First World War had immeasurably weakened Britain's position, such that the pre-war exchange rate against gold was completely inappropriate. His decision led to deflation and industrial unrest (as employers tried to cut wages) that prompted the general strike of 1926, the only such event in British history. Britain's economy only really recovered when it left the gold standard in 1931.

Mr Trump is making a similar mistake. Any hopes of returning the US to a golden age of manufacturing employment are doomed. Factory jobs have been declining, as a proportion of total employment, across the western world, even in Germany which has run consistent trade surpluses (where the value of exports exceeds that of imports).

If there are similarities between the mistakes of Trump and Churchill, there are also big differences. With the exception of Keynes, most experts in 1925 urged Churchill to rejoin the gold standard. Most modern economists would advise Mr Trump against his trade policies – but he relies on his own instincts and the support of a narrow coterie of acolytes. Worst of all, Churchill's policy mainly did damage to his own economy, but Trump's approach is causing turmoil both in the US and in the rest of the world.

Stop the world, Trump wants to get off

An elaborate system of global trade has been created since the Second World War. Raw materials, components, finished goods and services now move across national borders with increasing ease and frequency. Almost any resident of western Europe, the US or the Anglosphere (Australia, Britain, Canada and New Zealand) will have grown up in a world where they could pick from a range of global products. Indeed, trade is even more free than when Keynes wrote of the world before 1914: 'The inhabitant of London could order by telephone, sipping his morning tea in bed, the various products of the whole earth, in such quantity as he might see fit, and reasonably expect their early delivery upon his doorstep.'[3]

Arthur C. Clarke, the science fiction author, wrote that 'Any sufficiently advanced technology is indistinguishable from magic.' It is not magic that fills our homes with goods from around the world, but the result of a trading system to which few of us give much daily thought. These words are being typed on a Samsung laptop, which may have been assembled in South Korea but on its website, Samsung Electronics lists 100 different suppliers from many different countries.[4] And the laptop will have been brought to Britain by ship or plane and then transported, first to a warehouse and then to the retailer, by truck. The ships, planes, trucks, warehouse and retail store will have been built by companies with their own long chain of suppliers. Just typing this sentence probably required inputs from hundreds of thousands of people.

Apple currently uses 187 suppliers across twenty-eight countries to make the iPhone.[5] These are not relationships that can be picked up overnight and dropped back into the US. Trying to deconstruct a supply chain this intricate is like asking someone who has baked a cake to turn it back into eggs, flour, sugar, butter and baking soda.

This system of global trade is not the result of any individual's plan but arose from decades of trial and error, as businesses sought the best and cheapest ways to bring their goods to market. Just as evolution means those animals which adapt to the environment are most likely to survive, global trade means companies must adjust their supply chains to prosper. Governments have certainly been involved in the process, especially through deals to encourage greater trade, but the network has largely been created by companies operating within a free market.

This wave of globalisation has had enormous positive effects, with wealth spreading out from Europe and its former settler colonies to the rest of the world. The proportion of the world's citizens living in extreme poverty has dropped from 38 per cent in 1990 to 8.5 per cent in 2024.[6] As prosperity has spread, global life expectancy at birth has risen from 32 years in 1900 to 46 in 1950 and 73 years today.[7]

Back in the 1980s, the Republicans under President Ronald Reagan made much of their free-market principles and belittled the Democrats for their belief in government intervention. All that has changed. What could be more interventionist than dictating to companies where they should source their supplies? But that is what President Trump, with his 145 per cent tariffs on China, tried to do. He looked at the global trading system and, like a Marvel character shouting 'Hulk, smash!', vowed to destroy it.

Ironically, much of the immediate damage will be felt in the US. By setting a 145 per cent tariff on Chinese goods, in particular, Mr Trump effectively imposed an embargo on his own economy. If the word 'embargo' strikes a chord, that is because it is a familiar wartime tactic. Britain and France tried to impose an embargo on Germany in the First World War and Germany used its U-boats to cut off vital imports to the UK. This was an effort to defeat the enemy, not, to adapt Mr Trump's phrase, a way of 'making Britain great again'.

Within the first few weeks of Mr Trump's policy, shipments from China slumped. In many areas, like children's toys, China is the main supplier so the risk was that presents under the Christmas tree would be in short supply. Mr Trump, in a nod to Charles Dickens's Scrooge, said that children would have 'two dolls instead of thirty dolls' and they would cost a 'couple of bucks more'. In a neat summation of the whole policy, the comedian Mike Drucker tweeted that 'Your family will have less, but it will be more expensive.'[8]

Other sectors such as footwear manufacturing also warned that the sheer scale of the tariffs would lead to closed businesses, lost jobs, higher prices and shortages on shelves. There was simply no prospect that production could be moved back to the US in any realistic timescale. Indeed the footwear industry pointed out that Mr Trump had even placed a tariff on the machinery and materials needed to make footwear in the US.[9] This is not, to say the least, an example of joined-up thinking.

All these warnings prompted Mr Trump's retreat in May, a retreat that did not involve any concessions by China (which simply dropped its retaliatory tariffs). But the effects will linger. It will take time to replace the shipments that should have arrived in April or early May. Even the revised 30 per cent tariff will make some goods a lot more expensive.

But the broader point is that businesses cannot rest easy. They do not know what will happen when the ninety-day suspension periods expire (the global one is set to end in July, as this book is being published, and the China suspension in August). There is also the risk that Mr Trump will switch his attention to a new sector, like computer chips, and lob a grenade into its trading systems. Like a spouse who has found out that their partner has been unfaithful, companies will be braced for the next betrayal.

Tariffs are a blunt instrument

Even if US policymakers are worried about their trade deficit (when imports exceed exports), the blame does not lie with foreign tariffs. The tariff rates imposed by other countries have been steadily falling over time (the trade-weighted average for the EU in 2024 was 2.7 per cent and for China 3 per cent).[10] Tariffs started to fall significantly after 1991, a year in which the US ran a trade surplus. So if tariffs are the factor blocking the export of US goods now, how come they weren't a problem back then?

A country that imposes tariffs generally makes things worse for itself. An academic study that examined the effect of tariffs in more than 150 countries over a fifty-year period found that tariff increases were followed by adverse effects on output and productivity that were economically and statistically significant. Tariff increases were also followed by higher unemployment and greater inequality.[11] They are self-inflicted wounds.

The people who voted for Mr Trump may argue that, whatever the academics might say, globalisation hasn't worked for them. The standard of living of the ordinary worker has barely risen, jobs are less secure, and goods have become less affordable. As the book will point out, these developments weren't inevitable; other countries exposed to globalisation are more equal than the US, have better rights for their workers and stronger social safety nets. And trade with China can hardly be the main culprit when real wages began stagnating in 1973, long before China became a significant part of the global trading system.

But the main counter-argument is that the Trump plan won't help. It is a little like a patient with a persistent stomach ache who has despaired of over-the-counter remedies, and decided to check in with a private clinic for minor surgery, only to find that the surgeon in the operating theatre is Elon Musk with a chainsaw.

This book will explain why Trump's economic programme is misguided and will do a lot more economic harm than good. It will argue several points:

- Trade deficits are not disastrous, particularly for the US which finds it easy to attract international investors. The US deficit is driven more by the structure of the domestic economy than by the actions of foreign economies.
- If the aim is to cut the trade deficit, then Mr Trump's tax cuts for the wealthy will drive up the budget deficit and thus make the trade deficit worse.
- Tariffs are initially paid by importers, not by foreign

countries, and are mostly absorbed by domestic businesses or passed on to consumers. They make no sense in an era of global supply chains and will lead to higher prices and potential shortages of goods.

- A decline of manufacturing jobs has occurred across the developed world over many decades, even in countries with trade surpluses, and has a stronger link to automation than trade practices.
- US companies buy goods from overseas because they are cheaper (or not available in the home market). The manufacturing sector has switched its focus to higher-value goods. Trying to force domestic production back into low-value goods like toys or clothes will reduce productivity and, in any case, businesses will find it hard to attract the workers.
- The burden of higher tariffs will fall on lower-income consumers, either through tariffs, or because domestically made goods will be more expensive. Meanwhile tariff revenues will be used to justify a tax cut for the wealthy.

Furthermore, the way that economic policy has been carried out, with its arbitrary announcements and reversals, is itself incredibly damaging. Businesses do not know where to invest until the tariff rates settle so they will pause investment altogether. Andy Haldane, the former chief economist of the Bank of England, says the most persistent impact of Mr Trump will be to increase economic uncertainty, as his policies follow a long list of shocks from the great financial crisis through Covid and Russia's invasion of Ukraine.

Nor is the damage done by Trump's policies confined to trade. His assault on the independence of the Federal Reserve, the US central bank, led to a brief loss of confidence in the dollar and the safety of Treasury bonds. The cost of government borrowing rose again in mid-May when it became clear that Mr Trump intended to slash taxes, substantially increasing the budget deficit.[12]

Diluting the independence of the Fed is a great risk since investors tend to rely on the central bank to constrain governments which risk inflation by running big budget deficits. Investors might react by selling the dollar, pushing up the price of imports even further. When bond yields rise, the US government must pay more to service its debt, worsening its budget deficit. Another risk is that Mr Trump's attacks on US universities, a key source of research and development, threatens to weaken the long-term growth prospects of the US economy.

Finally, there is no sign that Mr Trump has a plan to replace the global system he has been smashing. This system emerged after 1945 as the US led an effort to rebuild the global economy after the Great Depression and the Second World War. Far-sighted US leaders, such as Harry Truman and George Marshall, sent aid to rebuild the European economies, helped Japan to recover and slowly dismantled the protectionist barriers that had been erected between the two world wars. The result was thirty years of unparalleled economic growth across the western world. This is the age that Trump voters are harking back to, but it was marked by liberalisation of trade and high taxes on the wealthy, not by increasing protectionism or tax cuts for billionaires.

Of course, this improvement in living standards in the developed world has stalled, particularly in the wake of the 2007–9 financial crisis. But Trump's plans will worsen the problem, not solve it. The 2 April version of the Trump tax could have sent the US into a Trump slump. Within weeks of the announcement of his planned tariffs, economic forecasters, including the authoritative International Monetary Fund, were slashing their forecasts for global economic growth, with US estimates taking the biggest hit.

Higher tariffs will mean higher consumer prices, and thus a pick-up in US inflation. That will make it harder for the Fed to conduct monetary policy. Should it cut interest rates to cushion the economy and risk stoking inflation? Or refrain from cutting rates in a bid to control inflation and risk an economic slowdown?

Some believe that Mr Trump is just using a tactic of maximum pressure. He will win some token concessions from other countries, declare victory and then retreat. The problem with this optimism is twofold. The first is that, if Mr Trump has any virtues, patience is not one of them. He will see something in the news that annoys him and after a tirade on social media, announce some new restrictions. Indeed, this happened in late May when he announced the doubling (to 50 per cent) of tariffs on steel and aluminium imports.

The second problem is that the damage has already been done. The global trading system was built with the help of international treaties and collective bodies, such as the General Agreement on Tariffs and Trade (GATT) and the World Trade Organization (WTO), that tried to develop global rules and settle disputes in an orderly fashion. Under the WTO's most favoured nation rule, countries must be treated equally; offer a sweetheart deal to one country and you must offer it to all. All this has been replaced by the whims of one man; the WTO has been effectively neutered.

Even if other countries make a deal with the US, they know that high tariffs could be reimposed at a moment's notice. The 'deal' announced with the UK in May was a classic example; just five pages long and incorporating a statement, on page 1, that it was not a legally binding agreement.[13]

A contract with Mr Trump is only valid until the president changes his mind; Mexico and Canada, which signed deals with the US in his first term, have discovered this to their cost. So much of economic activity depends on trust. When a purchaser buys goods from a supplier, they must trust that the goods will be delivered and that they will be of the desired quality. The supplier must trust that they will be paid. If they lack that trust, they will be less willing to make a deal. Changing the terms of the deal in the middle of the transaction by, for example, suddenly imposing tariffs, undermines trust significantly.

Mark Carney, the former governor of the Bank of England who became Canadian prime minister because of a perception that he could stand up to Trump, summed up the problem when he said: 'The system of global trade anchored on the United States is over. The eighty-year period when the United States embraced the mantle of global economic leadership is over. While this is a tragedy, it is also the new reality.'

Mr Carney's concerns raise a much broader point. The way in which the US exercised power after 1945 created an informal American empire, in which other democratic countries were happy to accept US hegemony. Broadly speaking, they adopted many items of American culture from its rock music through its movies through to its fast-food chains. While other democratic nations did not always approve of US foreign policy, in Vietnam or Iraq for example, they did not feel threatened by it. When the US wanted to act, it could count on other nations to join its gang; when it developed new goods, it had a ready market.

By declaring 'America first', and bullying its allies, Mr Trump has dissolved this informal empire. This is bad news for democracy in general. After 1945, there was, at least in the democratic world, a liberal international order; as the historian Timothy Garton Ash notes, the president 'is now tearing down what remains of the edifice with unparalleled speed and recklessness'.[14]

Mr Trump's approach also undermines the image of the US as the embodiment of the liberal democratic system. He bypasses Congress, attacks the courts and the free press, and only believes in elections when he wins them. This book is mainly concerned with trade policy but Mr Trump's authoritarianism, by eroding US soft power, has an economic impact too.

The world has got used to the president's extraordinary style, which involves sending out messages in block capitals that insult allies or threaten to annex their territory. But it is still remarkable. Any other president who called the Federal Reserve chairman a 'major loser' would, in the past, have been denounced by the corporate titans of Wall Street. Although the financiers don't protest (probably out of fear), Trump's style still undermines investor and business confidence, both vital for long-term prosperity. The economic consequences of Mr Trump are still unfolding, and the courts may yet bring the most damaging parts of his programme to a complete halt. But the risks are that he will destroy a global system that has brought benefits to billions.

1

WHERE THERE IS ORDER, LET THERE BE CHAOS

'Trade wars are good and easy to win.'

President Donald Trump, 2018

'Here's my guess. Never in human history has a whimsical decision by a single person destroyed so much wealth.'

Arindrajit Dube, Provost professor of economics,
University of Massachusetts Amherst, April 2025

In the first 100 days of his administration in 1933, Franklin D. Roosevelt stabilised the US banking system, introduced regulations to reduce the chance of a future stock-market crash, set up one scheme to prop up crop prices and another to find work for the unemployed, and created the Tennessee Valley Authority to control flooding and provide electricity. The result was that he restored confidence to a citizenry suffering from the Great Depression, declaring that 'the only thing we have to fear is fear itself'.

In the first 100 days of Donald Trump's second term, he took an axe to the global trading system, laid off vital public employees, cut funding for scientific research, threatened to annex the territory of a long-standing ally, prompted a decline in consumer confidence and caused alarm in significant parts of US industry. He took an economy that had grown 2.8 per cent in the previous year and brought it to a halt. Immigrants were snatched off the street and sent to prison in El Salvador with no judicial process. The aggressive treatment of those holding visas discouraged many tourists from visiting the US while academics, and even Wall Street financiers,[1] fell silent in case they faced retaliation. His major achievement was thus fear itself.

This book is mostly concerned with analysing the trade policy, rather than the broader set of policies, of the second Trump administration. And it is worth recounting the trade policy steps undertaken, just in the time between his 20 January inauguration and the end of May 2025.

1 February Trump announced 25 per cent tariffs on imports from Canada and Mexico (tearing up an agreement made in his first term), and 10 per cent on China.

3 February The Canadian and Mexican tariffs were suspended.

4 March The Canadian and Mexican tariffs were reinstated, and an additional 10 per cent imposed on China.

12 March Tariffs of 25 per cent were levied on all steel and aluminium imports.

26 March Announced 25 per cent tariffs on all imports of cars and car parts.

2 April Unveiled a wide range of levies on imported goods from around the world, using a formula based on bilateral trade deficits, with a maximum of 50 per cent. Imposed a base tariff of 10 per cent goods from all countries – bar Russia and North Korea.

9 April The formula-based tariffs were suspended for ninety days, leaving a base rate of 10 per cent, but China was hit with an additional 84 per cent of tariffs because it had retaliated. After a further Chinese response, total tariffs on Chinese goods were raised to 145 per cent.

11 April Some electronic goods and components were exempted from the punitive levies imposed on China, although a 20 per cent tariff on such goods remained.

29 April Exemptions and tariff reductions were offered to car manufacturers.

5 May Announced a plan to impose a 100 per cent tariff on all foreign-made films.

8 May Announced a trade deal with the UK. The UK lowers tariffs on agricultural products and gets some relief on cars and steel. The 10 per cent base tariff on British goods remained.

12 May After talks with China, the retaliatory tariffs were suspended for ninety days. This still left the US levying a 30 per cent tariff on China (down from 145 per cent) and China 10 per cent on the US (down from 125 per cent).

16 May Said that instead of negotiating deals with 150 countries, he would send letters to tell nations what 'they'll be paying to do business in the United States'. This suggested a return to something like the 2 April formula.

23 May Threatened to levy a 50 per cent tariff on EU goods on 1 June and to put a 25 per cent tariff on Apple's iPhones if production does not move to the US.

25 May Postponed the 50 per cent tariffs on the EU.

28 May US Court of International Trade rules that the president exceeded his power in imposing broad tariffs. The administration immediately appealed.

30 May Doubled the tariff on steel and aluminium to 50 per cent.

The above list only covers the actual policy announcements made. It would need to be a lot longer to cover the threats made on social media, the leaks from within the administration about future policy directions, and the boasts about the number of countries eager to make a deal with the US.

Formula is too formal a word for it

The best evidence that these policy changes were not part of a strategic plan came with the 'formula' used to calculate the tariffs announced on 2 April. Before the announcement, the White House had hinted at a complicated calculation of tariff and non-tariff barriers, including currency manipulation, regulation and taxes. But what emerged was nothing so analytical.

Instead, the calculation started with the US's 2024 trade balance in goods with a wide variety of countries and territories. This trade balance was then divided by the country's exports to the US and the result was deemed to be the level of 'tariffs' applied by the foreign nation. So, if the US had a trade deficit of $500m with Ruritania and imported $1bn worth of goods from that country, Ruritania was deemed to have a tariff rate of 50 per cent. That rate was then halved (Mr Trump described this as 'being kind') to get the US's new tariff rate; so 25 per cent in the fictional case of Ruritania. There was an exception to this rule, however. Even if the US had a trade surplus with another nation, that country still faced a tariff of 10 per cent.

James Surowiecki, the journalist who wrote the 2004 book *The Wisdom of Crowds*, seems to have been the first to spot this simplistic calculation method. However, when the White House released the details, the formula looked a lot more sophisticated because it incorporated some Greek letters. These additional terms were the elasticity of import demand with respect to import prices, and the elasticity of import prices with respect to tariffs.[2] It is perfectly reasonable to include these terms in a trade calculation as you would expect both demand and prices to adjust when tariffs are imposed. In the Trump formula, these two numbers were multiplied together, and the product was used as a divisor.

However, the Trump formula assumed an elasticity of import demand of 4 and an elasticity of import prices of 0.25, or a quarter. Multiplying four by a quarter results in an answer of one, and dividing by one means the number stays the same. So these 'sophisticated' additions to the calculations made no difference to the result. In practical terms, it was back to the trade balance divided by the country's exports.

Incidentally, the Trump administration cited some academic work as justification for the formula. But one of the academics behind the work said it had been cited in error.[3] In fact, the elasticity of import prices with respect to tariffs is almost 1. So the product of the two new terms should have been 4, not 1. As a result, the Trump formula should really have divided all its calculations by four. Even on the basis of its own reasoning, the Trump tariffs were *four times too high*. Had the formula been used correctly, the maximum tariff rate paid by any country would have been just over 13 per cent.[4]

This was only one of the many ways in which the formula was stupid. For a start, it focused on bilateral deficits (those with single nations) rather than the overall trade shortfall. The implied aim was for the US to have balanced trade with every other nation on the planet. This makes no sense in economic terms. In particular, it imposed harsh terms on poor countries in Asia and Africa.

Take Bangladesh, which has a GDP per capita of around $2,500 and mainly exports apparel to the US. It faced a tariff of 37 per cent for the 'crime' of supplying Americans with cheap clothes. Those clothes are cheap because Bangladeshi wages are much lower than those in the US (along with harsher working conditions). And since its wages are low its citizens don't have the money to buy the more high-value items that the US specialises in exporting. For Bangladesh to have a trade surplus with the US is perfectly rational.

Lesotho has a GDP per capita of only $900. Its biggest export to the US is diamonds, since it has one of the largest open-pit diamond mines in the world. In contrast, the US has virtually no natural diamonds (it does produce synthetic versions). So the US imports diamonds (plus cheap apparel) from Lesotho. Nearly all Lesotho's imports come from South Africa (which completely surrounds it) and, in any case, the citizens of Lesotho have insufficient income to afford many of the goods the US exports. The net result is that, in return for making brides-to-be happy with glittering diamonds, Lesotho was hit with a 50 per cent tariff, the highest of any country.

Secondly, there was nothing 'reciprocal' about these tariffs at all. Lesotho imposes zero or very little tariffs on US goods.[5] Brazil does impose tariffs and other barriers on US goods; before Trump's announcement, Capital Economics calculated that it should face a reciprocal rate of 28 per cent.[6] But because the US has a trade surplus with Brazil, the South American country only faced a tariff of 10 per cent, a fifth of the levy imposed on Lesotho.

A third problem was that the US formula focused only on

goods, not services. As will be discussed in the next chapter, services are more important in terms of economic activity than goods and they are an area where the US runs a trade surplus. For example, Bermuda, which is a hub for international finance and insurance, exports a lot of services to the US, and has an overall trade surplus with it. But since it doesn't have a trade surplus *in goods* with the US, it was only hit with a 10 per cent tariff. Similarly, the EU and Switzerland import a lot of services from the US and would have faced a much lower tariff rate than the punitive levels originally imposed on 2 April had services been included in the calculations.[7]

Fourth, trade balances with countries vary from year to year. *The New York Times* found that, had the tariffs been calculated on the basis of 2023 numbers instead of 2024, Saudi Arabia would have suffered a higher levy than the 10 per cent imposed, because the Saudis had a surplus with the US in 2023. Were the Saudis cheating in 2023 but suddenly not doing so in 2024?

Finally, in further proof of the slapdash nature of the whole exercise, the formula imposed a tariff on the uninhabited Heard and McDonald Islands, a remote group of islands inhabited predominantly by penguins. This inspired lots of internet memes involving flocks of penguins 'protesting' against the levy. Trump's commerce secretary, Howard Lutnick, who is apparently unembarrassable, defended the decision, saying 'If you leave anything off the list, the countries that try to basically arbitrage America go through those countries to us.'[8] The Heard and McDonald Islands are a two-week boat ride from Australia and have not been visited by humans for ten years.

Reports suggest that the simplistic formula was selected

by Trump himself, just three hours before the announcement was made.[9] That would certainly explain why the president held up a clunky sign at the conference to illustrate his plan, which reporters struggled to read.

So, to sum up, the formula was based on a ridiculous premise, was not reciprocal, only included part of the trade relationship with other countries, used an arbitrary time period, used the wrong numbers for price elasticity, and had the ridiculous consequence of taxing non-existent trade with penguins.

Given all this, it is not surprising that a liberal economist like Paul Krugman would describe the approach as 'something thrown together by a junior staffer with only a couple of hours' notice'.[10] But in an unusual confluence, the conservative American Enterprise Institute also dismissed the formula as having 'no foundation in either economic theory or trade law'.[11]

Flooding the zone

The blizzard of announcements from the administration has provoked an intensive search for some underlying rationale. Among Trump's supporters, it is often claimed that the president is playing three-dimensional chess while the rest of the world is playing checkers. It certainly seems that acting swiftly was part of the administration's plan, since there have been similarly rapid moves to cut civil service jobs and deport immigrants. Simultaneous action on several fronts is a way of wrongfooting opponents and distracting the media, or 'flooding the zone with shit', as Steve Bannon, an adviser to Trump in his first term, describes it.

But this is surely a moment for using Occam's razor,

which states that the simplest explanation is most likely to be correct. The rapid changes of policy demonstrate not that there was a cunning master plan, but that the Trump administration was making it up as it went along. The term 'sanewashing' has been applied to journalists who attempted to find a coherent strategy among the mess.

Take the idea of a Mar-a-Lago Accord, the term used for a plan suggested by Stephen Miran, chair of the Council of Economic Advisers. The name echoes the Plaza Accord of the 1980s, when the US persuaded other countries, notably Japan, to let their currencies strengthen against the dollar. The idea was that a stronger yen and weaker dollar would make Japanese imports less attractive to Americans, and American exports more appealing to consumers in other nations, thereby reducing the US trade deficit.

Miran's plan involved leveraging America's economic and military power to persuade other countries to 'correct' their trade surpluses with the US and provide its government with cheap finance (among other things). But the plan involved raising tariffs gradually in order not to upset the markets. Instead Trump pushed up tariffs rapidly and massively on 2 April, and prompted market turmoil. The administration then suspended many of the most punitive tariffs on 9 April. This was not the kind of 'credible forward guidance' that Miran suggested.

Clearly, there was nothing sophisticated about the formula at all. Instead of a game of three-dimensional chess, the president was playing darts with a javelin; the only plausible outcome was the destruction of the board, and great danger to everyone around him.

Supporters claimed, as evidence of Mr Trump's 'genius', that nations were queueing up to negotiate away the tariffs. They took their cue from the president himself when he said, at a dinner for the National Republican Congressional Committee on 8 April, 'I'm telling you, these countries are calling us up, kissing my ass. They are dying to make a deal.'[12] The administration referred to 'more than seventy-five' countries that had approached the US to negotiate.[13] Since the White House refused to provide a list of these nations, the claim had an element of the schoolboy boast: 'I really have a girlfriend but you won't know her because she's at another school.'

Some countries, like Vietnam, did offer to talk. Under the spurious Trump formula, Vietnam was facing a 46 per cent tariff. This rate was a fantasy that was unrelated to actual Vietnamese trade policy. Whatever deal Vietnam agreed to strike, there is no way that its trade surplus with the US would disappear, unless the US placed a complete embargo on Vietnamese imports. The UK also did a deal with Mr Trump, although as already noted, it was a non-binding agreement covering only a limited number of sectors.

Proper trade agreements take years to negotiate, not a few weeks (the creation of the Trans-Pacific Partnership of twelve countries took seven years). So, it was perhaps unsurprising that, on 16 May, Mr Trump announced that he would simply tell other nations what tariff they would have to pay. This implied a return to higher rates than the 10 per cent base level set on 9 April. The future of trade seems to look like a bewildering patchwork, rather than a coherent whole.

This lack of coherence explains why, like most economists, other countries have struggled to understand what the US actually wants out of this process. As will be discussed in Chapter 4, one apparent desire is to create more manufacturing jobs, a return to some golden age of manual labour.

But that is far from the only goal. Indeed, the justification for the initial set of tariffs on China, Canada and Mexico (back on 1 February) was that the two latter countries had failed to do enough to stop illegal immigration and that all three countries were responsible for the flow of the highly addictive drug fentanyl into the US. This was particularly hard on Canada, since just 43 pounds of the drug was seized at the northern border in 2024, less than 1 per cent of the amount confiscated by customs officials at the southern border.[14]

Another potential aim is to raise revenue. Peter Navarro, the president's trade adviser, suggested that the tariffs could raise $600bn a year while Mr Trump floated the idea that tariff revenue could even replace the federal income tax for those earning less than $200,000.[15] Both suggestions are implausible (see Chapter 3). And if imports were high enough to raise substantial amounts of money, that suggests the failure of one of the administration's other priorities. Companies would not have moved their goods production back to the US.

Finally, Mr Trump has also used tariffs (or the threat of them) to exert his will over foreign nations. In January, when the Colombian president complained about the deportation of migrants to his country, the president threatened 25 per cent tariffs on Colombian imports until he backed down. It is possible that Mr Trump likes tariffs so much as they are easy to impose and they force other nations to beg him for deals. It is an exertion of dominance that Mr Trump, who perceives himself to be an alpha male, enjoys.

The trade strategy can therefore be seen as part of a wider attempt to exert American power. It ties in with the president's clear 'dictator envy' which prompts him to show much greater admiration for Vladimir Putin than for the leaders of the US's traditional allies. Mr Trump has clearly sided with Russia over Ukraine in his attempts to settle the war. It seems that the president sees Russia, like the US, as a great power, and that gives it the right to control countries within its sphere of influence. Whereas the Biden administration supported Ukraine as a fellow democracy that had been invaded, the Trump White House seems to have been guided by the Thucydides quote 'the strong do what they can, and the weak suffer what they must'.

The same philosophy drives Mr Trump's threats to seize control of the Panama Canal, annex Greenland (currently governed by Denmark, a NATO ally), to incorporate Canada (a threat that spurred a surge of Canadian patriotism) and even, most absurdly, to turn the devastated Gaza Strip into a Middle Eastern riviera. By expanding US territory, Mr Trump thinks he will enter the pantheon of America's greatest presidents and satisfy his ambition of being immortalised on Mount Rushmore.

This aggression is weakening the US's considerable soft power, as will be discussed in Chapter 6. 'Flooding the zone with shit' may confuse the media but it also confuses the US's allies. No one knows what Mr Trump will announce next and he simply can't be relied on as a partner, whether the issue is trade, defence or anything else.

Downmarket approach

This unpredictable behaviour also confuses the markets. Mr Trump boasted about the strong performance of the US stock market during his first term of office. In his second term, however, he hasn't seemed to mind when share prices fall, even when those declines were clearly a direct response to his tariff plans. In the two days after he announced his trade package, the S&P 500 lost $5tn in value.[16] Having said that the tariffs would 'Make America Wealthy Again', the decline in equity prices was the equivalent of a loss of nearly $15,000 for every US citizen.

In March, when the threat of tariffs was already starting to unnerve markets, Mr Trump had a grumpy explanation for the decline in share prices. 'Well, a lot of them are globalist countries and companies that won't be doing as well,' he said. 'Because we're taking back things that have been taken from us many years ago.'[17] (Globalist, a loaded term with an antisemitic history, is an insult often used by the US political right.)[18]

What seemed to change Mr Trump's mind was not the stock market, but the bond market. In the US, the Treasury bond market is the way that the government finances its budget deficit (along with shorter-term debt known as Treasury bills). James Carville, an adviser to President Bill Clinton, said in the 1990s that he wanted to be reincarnated as the bond market because then he could come back and intimidate everybody.

Most bonds are issued with a set interest rate, or coupon in the jargon, which is paid to investors until the debt is repaid (matures). While the coupon doesn't vary, bonds are tradable so their price changes all the time. So, a bond with a face value of 100 might see its price rise to 120, or drop to 80. Take a bond with a coupon of 5 per cent, i.e. $5 on every $100. If the price falls to $80, the income return is proportionately more than when the price was $100, and the income is proportionately less if the price rises to $120.

The relationship between the coupon and the bond price is known as the yield. The key thing to understand is that, as bond prices fall, yields rise and, as bond prices rise, yields fall. This matters because the US government, like many others, has a lot of debt. At the time of writing, it had $36.9tn of debt and in 2024, it spent more than $1.1tn in servicing that debt.[19] Over the course of any given year, much of the debt matures and must be refinanced. Higher yields mean that the cost of refinancing that debt will rise.

For many governments, this can become a vicious circle. As the cost of servicing debt rises, the government finds it harder to balance its budget. This means it must issue more debt, which means even higher interest payments and so on. Traditionally, the US government has not been affected by this problem. By the most commonly used measure, it has the largest economy in the world and the Treasury bond market is the most liquid global market. Investors regard Treasury bonds as being a 'safe haven' (admittedly, a tautology) and tend to park funds there when they are nervous. In 2008, when a financial crisis was in full swing – a crisis caused by irresponsible lending in the US housing market

– the yield on the thirty-year Treasury bond fell from 4.45 per cent at the start of the year to 2.7 per cent by the end.[20] A crisis that began in America had the effect of lowering the US government's borrowing costs.

The safety appeal of Treasury bonds normally means that when the stock market falls, as it did in the aftermath of Trump's 2 April announcement, Treasury bond prices rise (and yields fall). Shares look more risky, so buy bonds, goes the reasoning. But in early April 2025, that didn't happen; the yield on the ten-year Treasury bond rose from 3.9 per cent to 4.5 per cent in the week after 2 April, while the yield on the thirty-year bond rose from 4.4 per cent to top 5 per cent.[21]

It was this turbulence in the bond market that seemed to spook Scott Bessent, the Treasury secretary, and Howard Lutnick, the commerce secretary, who then persuaded Mr Trump to suspend the higher tariffs. According to the *Wall Street Journal*, Messrs Bessent and Lutnick waited for Peter Navarro to be in another meeting before they lobbied the president.[22] Bond yields duly dropped after Mr Trump delayed some of the tariffs on 9 April.

The hostile market reaction reminded some of Britain's experience in the autumn of 2022 when the government of Liz Truss slashed taxes, at a time of high inflation, with no clear plan to limit government borrowing. The financial turmoil played a large part in Ms Truss's departure from office, after the shortest-ever stint for a British prime minister.

Indeed, there was one other Truss parallel that was striking, and worrying. Normally, when Treasury bond yields are rising, the dollar goes up in value against other currencies. Higher bond yields means the dollar is offering a higher income to international investors, making holding the dollar more attractive. But in the week after 2 April, that didn't happen. The dollar fell, making this a triple vote of no confidence in economic policy: falling share prices, falling bond prices and a falling currency.

This combination, which became known as the 'sell America' trade, didn't last that long. But it was a worrying indicator that international investors might be losing their long-held confidence in American assets as the cornerstone of their portfolios. In the course of Mr Trump's first 100 days in office, John Authers of Bloomberg calculated that the dollar had dropped 10 per cent in trade-weighted terms, the worst start under any president since the 1970s when the currency lost its link to gold. It was also the worst stock-market performance in the first 100 days since Richard Nixon's second term, when the US was mired in stagflation.

Trump enthusiasts can point to the rally which reversed the stock market's losses in the second half of April and early May. But that rally was predicated on the notion that the 'reciprocal' tariffs announced on 2 April would not be reintroduced (after the ninety-day suspension) and that the suspension of the retaliatory tariffs imposed by the US and China would be permanent.

This enthusiasm masks an important point. It was Mr Trump's original suite of policies that forced the markets down and his retreat from those policies that allowed them to rebound. This is a bit like a chef serving his guests a meal that gives them food poisoning, and then claiming credit for calling an ambulance.

The stock market's willingness to forgive Mr Trump is so naive that it is almost touching. When he was elected in November 2024, share prices rose because investors thought he wouldn't actually impose the tariffs he'd promised constantly during the campaign. In late April and May, share prices recovered because they thought Mr Trump would drop tariffs in the end. Robert Armstrong of the *Financial Times* dubbed it the 'Taco theory' with the acronym standing for 'Trump Always Chickens Out'.[23] Judged by the president's anger when confronted with the term,[24] he could reimpose tariffs just to show that he is tough.

Risky business

Wall Street is, at best, an imperfect indicator of the health of the US economy. The economist Paul Samuelson once joked that the stock market had predicted nine of the last five recessions. But there were clear signs that business confidence had been affected by the tariff package. The New York Federal Reserve's Empire State manufacturing survey in April found that firms had become pessimistic about the outlook, with the future general business conditions index falling to its second-lowest level ever.[25] The May survey showed a further decline in activity.[26] The Federal Reserve Bank of Philadelphia's survey of manufacturing found that the proportion of businesses which planned to increase capital spending dropped from 39 per cent in January to just 2 per cent in April.[27] Note that this is the manufacturing sector, the very segment of the economy Mr Trump was supposedly aiming to help.

The tariffs seem set to have a significant impact on

international trade. This can be seen in the amount of container traffic leaving China to go to the US, which nearly halved in the weeks following the imposition of punitive tariffs.[28] As further evidence of the decline, Hapag-Lloyd, the German shipping group, said in April that 30 per cent of its sailings from China to the US had been cancelled[29] while the air freight industry said bookings from China were also down by around 30 per cent.[30] There was a rebound in container freight in May, once the most punitive tariffs were reduced, but that revival caused shipping costs to soar, a burden that could be passed on to consumers.[31]

In the first quarter of 2025, imports increased as companies raced to bring in goods ahead of the tariff package. Although this was widely reported as reducing GDP, it didn't. As the name suggests, gross domestic product only counts goods and services produced within the economy, so imports don't add or subtract from the number.[32] Those increased imports seem to have shown up largely as inventories, which rose by a rapid 2.25 per cent. But this effect may reverse in subsequent quarters, with unpredictable effects on growth.

Had the punitive tariffs been maintained, the consequences would have rippled through the economy. Truckers would have had fewer loads to transport from Los Angeles and other ports and eventually, fewer goods would have made it to the shopping malls. CBS reported that the chief executives of both Walmart and Target, two of America's biggest retailers, warned the president that the tariff regime could lead to empty shelves within a few weeks.[33]

Further evidence for potential problems came from

a survey by the US Toy Association, an industry group. Around 80 per cent of the toys sold in American shops are made in China.[34] The prospect of 145 per cent tariffs on Chinese goods was therefore completely prohibitive. A survey of members, published on 18 April, found that 87 per cent of mid-sized toy companies were delaying orders, 80 per cent were cancelling them and 45 per cent expected to go out of business within weeks or months. Toys for the holiday season are ordered as early as July, so even with 30 per cent tariffs on China, Mr Trump may turn out to be the Grinch who stole Christmas for lots of American kids.

More generally, corporate leaders can be forgiven for being completely confused. The suspension of the punitive China tariffs for just ninety days may mean there is another rush to order goods in case the 145 per cent tariff rates re-appear in August. This pattern of feast and famine makes life very disruptive for businesses.

The same problem afflicts Mr Trump's apparent strategic goal of bringing manufacturing back to the US. After 2 April, executives might have started to wonder whether they did need to move operations, as almost every low-cost manufacturing hub in the world was suffering a high tariff. But a week later, the global system was up-ended and a month later, there was the China deal. In each case, the hiatus was only for ninety days. In the face of these changes, the logical thing for businesses to do was nothing: to sit tight and find out what the final policy mix would be. That is bad for business investment. And if Mr Trump is trying to help the car industry, it is not working so far; on 29 April, General Motors suspended a share buy-back plan and then said, two days later, its costs from tariffs would be $4–5bn.[35,36] In May, Ford added it expected a $1.5bn hit to operating profits from Mr Trump's tariff plan.[37]

Small businesses are suffering just as badly. At the end of April, the US Chamber of Commerce wrote to Mr Bessent saying that it was 'hearing from small business owners every day who are seeing their ability to survive endangered by the recent increase in tariff rates'. The group called for 'immediate action to save America's small businesses and stave off a recession'. Specifically, the business group called for small businesses to be exempt from tariffs, for automatic exclusions where goods cannot be produced in the US and for other exclusions where it could be shown that the tariffs were a risk to employment.[38] That would remove tariffs in most cases.

What about the public? The confidence measure of the Conference Board, a research group, declined in the early months of Mr Trump's term. The March survey, before the tariff announcement, showed a big fall in sentiment about the economic outlook, and things were even worse in April when expectations fell to their lowest since 2011.[39] There was then a rebound in May after the partial retreat on the tariff policy.[40]

For the economy to grow, businesses must be confident enough to invest and expand and consumers must be willing to buy goods and services. Without that, an economy can stall rather like a sailing boat can get marooned in the absence of a helpful wind. In mid-April, after the suspension of the initial tariff programme, Goldman Sachs still estimated the probability of a US recession at 45 per cent while the International Monetary Fund, the international trade body set up in 1944 with the help of Keynes, put the odds at just under 40 per cent (the US took the biggest hit in its forecast,[41] although Goldman lowered the risk to 35 per cent after the temporary China deal).

To sum up, all the damage described in this chapter is a self-inflicted wound. As the old line from a horror movie goes, 'The call is coming from inside the house.'

It is, of course, possible that the May deal with China, and the court ruling later in the month, will presage the complete abandonment of Mr Trump's plans. Let us hope that does happen. But that would run counter to Mr Trump's entrenched positions on the benefits (or lack of them) of international trade, the subject of the next chapter.

2

TRADE IS THE ESSENCE OF MODERN LIFE

'Practical men, who believe themselves to be quite exempt from any intellectual influence, are usually the slaves of some defunct economist. Madmen in authority, who hear voices in the air, are distilling their frenzy from some academic scribbler of a few years back.'

John Maynard Keynes, *The General Theory of Employment, Interest and Money*

'It is the maxim of every prudent master of a family, never to attempt to make at home what it will cost him more to make than to buy. The tailor does not attempt to make his own shoes, but buys them from the shoemaker. The shoemaker does not attempt to make his own clothes, but employs a tailor.'

Adam Smith, *The Wealth of Nations*

Humans have been trading since before recorded history. Archaeologists have found evidence of trade in stone tools, between humans that lived in Africa, that date back 320,000 years.[1] Those tools were transported over a range of just 50 miles but by around 7000 BCE, obsidian, a black volcanic glass, was taken from central Turkey to Cyprus. The Mesopotamian civilisation that emerged around 3000 BCE traded goods in an area that covered the Persian Gulf, the Caucasus and the Indus valley.[2]

Along with this long-distance trade, there was plenty going on at a local level. Farmers swapped their crops for other goods, such as clothes or pots. And, of course, this kind of commerce still dominates today. When politicians talk of trade, they mean the exchange of goods and services that takes place across borders. But we all trade every day; it is the essence of human society.

Look around your home. How many items could you make if you really needed to, and had the time to do so? A tiny fraction. We develop an expertise in treating patients, cutting hair, teaching children (or writing books) and then trade the wages we earn for those goods and services we desire.

In his 1776 book *The Wealth of Nations*, Adam Smith described one of the key benefits of trade: specialisation. He used the example of a pin factory where all the different stages of production had been separated, thereby making the process much more efficient. But the reasoning also applies to the wider economy. We each undertake the activity that earns us the highest return (or gives us the greatest satisfaction), and the result is much greater prosperity than if we spent our days trying to grow our own food, make our own clothes and so on. (My woodworking teacher told me I was the worst pupil he had taught in forty years so I am very glad I do not have to sit on my own furniture.)

For much of human history, most trade was local. Long-distance trade was slower, and riskier, and tended to focus on high-value items. But the rewards could be great. Both the Roman and Mongolian empires recognised the prosperity that trade could bring and thus encouraged it and tried to protect it.

As Adam Smith recognised, what is true for an individual can also be true for a nation. Just as the cobbler is best at making shoes and the blacksmith iron tools, Portugal could be best at making wine and England at producing wool. Trade is not a zero-sum game in which one side must lose. To take Smith's example, the English end up with *both* wine and textiles; the Portuguese with textiles and wine.

But Smith was battling a school of thought called mercantilism, of which Mr Trump is a distant disciple. Mercantilism emerged with the modern state, with governments viewing wealth as the gold and silver in their Treasuries and in the hands of merchants they could tax. When a nation imported more than it exported, that meant it exchanged gold and silver for those imports, and the reserves of precious metal fell. By the mercantilists' logic, that meant the nation was worse off.

Smith argued that a nation's prosperity was driven not by its stocks of gold and silver, but by the goods and services it consumes and produces. Trade increases this flow of goods and services and should be encouraged, not restricted.

Smith's views were refined by the nineteenth-century economist David Ricardo. Smith argued that countries with an absolute advantage in an area should trade with each other (the England–Portugal wool–wine swap). But Ricardo said this was also true if countries had a comparative advantage. If country A produces washing machines 80 per cent as efficiently as country B, and cars 65 per cent as efficiently, it is better for country A to focus on washing machines and country B on cars. This concept created many more theoretical justifications for trade.

At the time Smith and Ricardo wrote their respective treatises, Britain was not really a free-trading nation; for example, under the Navigation Act, trade to and from the colonies could only be carried in British ships. In the nineteenth century, however, the country moved steadily in the direction of free trade. It had industrialised well before other nations, so it had a huge competitive advantage.

The first phase of globalisation

Although other nations than Britain still imposed tariffs on imports, the second half of the nineteenth century saw a massive expansion in global trade as railways and steamships slashed the time and costs needed to bring goods to market. These reduced costs overwhelmed the impact of tariffs and brought cheap food from the US and South America to Europe. This allowed the living standards of industrial workers to improve (something that hadn't happened in the first half of the nineteenth century when the scale of poverty inspired the writings of Karl Marx). This cheap food was bad news for European agriculture but meant that millions of farmworkers were inspired to emigrate to the US, the British colonies and South America, where they provided the labour that allowed those economies to expand.

The first great era of globalisation was cut short by the First World War. The interwar period started well for the US, but most of Europe did not experience the 'roaring twenties'. The British economy faced deflation and high unemployment (thanks, in part, to Churchill's gold-standard decision) and Germany suffered from hyperinflation. The 1930s were even worse as the Great Depression spread around the world. Trade plummeted; world exports were only half as large, as a percentage of GDP, in the late 1930s as they were in 1914.

When the democratic world tried to rebuild itself after 1945, it learned some of the lessons of the interwar period. Neither Japan nor West Germany was burdened with the kind of massive reparations that were imposed on Germany in the Versailles treaty of 1919. Indeed, the US made special efforts to rebuild both economies. The Marshall Plan of foreign aid from the US helped economies across western Europe to recover. In part, this aid was designed to head off the threat of communism, but the US also recognised that Europeans would make great customers for its industries. American leaders of the time were well aware that trade was not a zero-sum game. They signed up to the General Agreement on Tariffs and Trade (GATT), which came into effect in 1948, to reduce trade barriers.

Two groups of countries did not follow the path towards freer trade. The first was the Communist bloc, which excluded many foreign products. While the Soviet Union certainly managed to generate growth in heavy industries (such as steel), developed strong military forces and took an initial lead in the space race, its consumer sector languished. Its population gradually became aware that people in the US and western Europe enjoyed a higher standard of living while many Soviet goods, such as cars, were of inferior quality. When the Iron Curtain fell, much of eastern Europe joined the EU while Russia became an example of 'authoritarian capitalism' in which rich men controlled businesses at the whim of Vladimir Putin.

The other great communist power, China, made some disastrous economic decisions under Chairman Mao, such as the Great Leap Forward (1958–62) which resulted in widespread famine. The country's rise to prosperity only began under Deng Xiaoping, who took over in 1978. Using the precept that 'it doesn't matter whether the cat is black or white, as long as it catches mice', Deng gave farmers and businesses more freedom to plot their own path, and to keep some of their gains. Gradually, China became part of the global trading economy, with the result that hundreds of millions of its people escaped extreme poverty.

The second group of countries which followed a different path included India and many nations in Latin America, which opted for policies of 'import substitution industrialisation'. The underlying idea was that the western world was exploiting these countries by flooding them with manufactured imports, leaving them to focus on low-margin and volatile commodity production. Instead, developing nations aimed to exclude imports and build their own industries in areas such as cars and domestic appliances.

The problem with import substitution industrialisation is that it very easily leads to crony capitalism in which favoured businesses prosper safe in the knowledge that they cannot be undermined by foreign competition. The result is higher prices and inferior goods for domestic consumers. Such products are not good enough to compete in global markets.

By contrast, some of the success stories in Asia, such as Taiwan and South Korea, focused on generating more exports, rather than excluding imports. This was not a 'free market' story – there was a lot of government interference to boost the likes of Hyundai and Samsung – but the focus on a global market ensured that such companies became competitive. India started to liberalise in 1991, and has shown remarkable success in growing its economy, and reducing the poverty rate from 55 per cent to 16 per cent within fifteen years (the equivalent of 415 million people).[3] While the country retains protectionist instincts, it is much more focused on global trade than it was in the 1970s or 1980s.

Globalisation blooms

By the mid-1960s fifty countries had signed up to GATT, compared with the original twenty-three founding members. Like a snowball, the trading system picked up more speed, with successive rounds of negotiations lowering tariff rates. Even so, it wasn't until the 1970s that trade regained the share of global GDP that had existed before 1914. But from that point, it expanded rapidly as China and eastern Europe joined the global trading system. GATT itself was replaced by the World Trade Organization in 1995 and the WTO made the rules for trading more formal, including a mechanism for resolving disputes. By 2010 or so, trade had doubled its share of GDP relative to the pre-1914 era. World trade volumes today are around forty-five times higher in volume terms (and 382 times higher in value terms) than they were in 1950.[4]

In case there is any doubt, shifting towards free trade is good for an economy. A literature review by Douglas Irwin of Dartmouth College found that developing countries which eased trade barriers received a boost of 1–1.5 per cent of GDP a year, which had the cumulative impact of 15–20 per cent higher incomes over the course of a decade.[5]

To be fair, completely free trade has been rare in history. There are usually some sectors, notably defence, where countries want to ensure that they can count on domestic supply in an emergency. And there are some strategic industries that countries may not want to see pass into the hands of a geopolitical competitor. That was why Joe Biden, Mr Trump's predecessor, put tariffs on Chinese semiconductors and restricted the export to China of some advanced technology, such as high-end computer chips.[6]

But China (and Russia) are authoritarian states which can threaten the interests of the democratic world. There is no strategic threat from Canada or Mexico, two long-standing allies, let alone Britain, which has loyally backed the US in every war since Vietnam. Indeed, by initially imposing swingeing tariffs on countries all over the world on 2 April, Mr Trump enhanced the appeal to other nations of buddying up to China, which has a much steadier policymaking process.

Anti-globalisation

Opposition to globalisation started to coalesce in the 1990s, and initially focused on the power of multinational corporations and the poor treatment of workers in developing nations. This critique largely came from the left of politics. But two events shifted the thrust of criticism to politicians on the right. The first was the admission of China to the WTO in 2001, after a long negotiation during which China agreed to open up its markets.

The hope was that, once inside the WTO, China would gradually liberalise and, as a prosperous middle class emerged, loosen the hold of the Communist Party. Those hopes proved illusory. In the meantime, China's trade boomed and the country leapt from being the fourth-largest manufacturer in the world in 2000 to being top of the league in 2023, with a market share double the size of the US's.[7] This coincided with a loss of US manufacturing jobs in the early 2000s and explains much of the resentment towards China among the US public, and in Mr Trump's circle.

The second development that undermined support for globalisation was the financial crisis of 2007–9. The financial sector was liberalised in the 1980s and 1990s, during a period dubbed the 'great moderation' when inflation was low and recessions were rare. Throughout these years, interest rates fell and share prices boomed making many financiers rich. Since they were wealthy, it was common to assume that financiers were smart (rather than lucky). Few politicians wanted to interfere with this boom, not least because bankers and fund managers in the US made hefty campaign contributions.

The crash of 2007 shattered the illusion. 'Smart' bankers had lent money to so-called 'NINJA' borrowers: people with no income, job or assets. The banks bundled together these lower-quality loans into complex securities without fully understanding the risks and unknowingly overstretched their balance sheets. When a liquidity crunch hit, these 'masters of the universe', as the author Tom Wolfe once labelled them, had no one to turn to but the government for help. And the government, worried about the kind of banking collapse that sparked the Great Depression, had to respond. Billions upon billions of dollars were pledged to bail out very rich financiers from a disaster of their own creation.

The result was outrage. The bankers had made stupid mistakes, only to be rescued by the taxpayer without a single person going to jail. Voters blamed 'the elite' for the mess, lumping together all the politicians of the centre-right and centre-left who had supported globalisation and the bailout of finance. Anyone who promised a radical change, whether it was Donald Trump or the British politicians who backed Brexit, was campaigning on fertile ground.

A narrative emerged on the right. Globalisation, and mass immigration, were part of a 'plot' by the 'elite', a term used to describe almost the entire educated, professional class. This elite was internationally mobile and unlikely to lose their jobs in the face of either international competition or immigration. The poor old working classes, by contrast, would bear the brunt of globalisation.

But while that narrative gained traction in the West, many countries in the developing world had a completely different view of globalisation. In the early 1960s, South Korea had a lower per capita income than Haiti or Yemen.[8] By 2016, the government's industrial strategy had turned it into the eleventh-largest economy in the world thanks to a focus on international trade; exports more than doubled as a share of its GDP between 1995 and 2012.[9] Vietnam recovered from the turmoil of the long war with the US that ended in 1975, launching a series of reforms in 1986 that enabled GDP per capita to jump from less than $700 in 1986 to almost $4,500 in 2023. The proportion of Vietnam's population in extreme poverty dropped from 14 per cent in 2010 to under 4 per cent in 2023.[10] All this was achieved through a focus on exports including electronic components and textiles.

Although their export orientation was the same, the political directions of the two countries were quite different. South Korea, which was invaded by North Korea in 1950, had an authoritarian regime until 1987, when it began to adopt democracy. It became a poster child for the benefits of capitalism, given its prosperity relative to its poverty-stricken neighbour. Vietnam still has a communist government.

How are these two countries supposed to react when the US, which had previously encouraged trading links, imposes high tariffs as Mr Trump did on 2 April (25 per cent for South Korea and 46 per cent for Vietnam)? While the US turns its back on such countries, China is eager to establish stronger ties or links with other nations. Its economy is still growing fast, making trade deals potentially lucrative.

The influence of the developed world is felt not just through trade, but through aid. So the slashing of the US foreign aid budget under Elon Musk's Department of

Government Efficiency represents a further loss of US soft power and a gap that China is only too happy to fill. The goal of closing the trade deficit is causing an awful lot of collateral damage.

What drives trade surplus and deficits

Mr Trump has talked about the US being 'ripped off' and 'pillaged' by other nations in terms of trade. But how in practice is this supposed to happen? One obvious reason why US businesses and consumers buy imports is because they are cheaper. Some argue that China is selling the goods too cheaply. But is this 'ripping off' America? It is an odd concept in any other walk of life. Imagine saying 'Hey, the local supermarket has cut the price of potatoes by 50 per cent. They are really ripping us off.'

A stronger line of complaint is that, while the US and other nations freely accept Chinese exports, China does not respond in kind. Foreign companies are shut out of the country by a series of government regulations. Those who try to get round the problem by allying with a Chinese partner risk losing their valuable intellectual property. There is undoubtedly justification for these complaints. But that is not the same as saying, as was the case with the Trump tariff formula, that *all* other nations are treating the US unfairly. As mentioned in Chapter 1, the 2 April tariff rates had no intellectual rationale; even countries with which the US has a trade surplus were hit with a 10 per cent tariff.

Mr Trump seems to take the mercantilist view that exports are good and imports are bad. But that is a very strange way to look at the world. It is a bit like saying that going to work to earn a salary is good but spending the money in a shop is bad. We take jobs so we can afford to buy things and, by the same token, we export goods and services so we can consume imports. Those imports may be things that can't be produced at home (diamonds, bananas), of a better quality than can be made at home (French wine or Scotch whisky) or are simply cheaper (such as electronics made in Asia).

The balance of trade in goods is only part of the flow of payments between a country and the rest of the world, captured in a nation's current account. This consists of a number of elements: trade in goods, trade in services, net income from abroad (salaries, dividends etc.) and current transfers, which include remittances sent home by people working abroad, foreign aid and donations. These elements may be moving in quite different directions. The UK, for example, has long experienced a trade deficit in goods but this has been partly offset by a surplus in services. The same is true for the US. While President Trump complains about the trade deficit in the goods the US makes, he does not mention the surplus in the services the US sells. If the goods deficit indicates that other countries are cheating the US, does the services surplus show that the US is cheating other nations? And if not, why not?

If a country runs a current account deficit, that means it is paying more to foreigners than it is receiving in return. The result is that those foreigners have claims on the deficit country. These claims may be in the form of bank deposits, equities (shares), government bonds or property. Or it may involve an overseas company building a factory in the deficit country, which is known as foreign direct investment or FDI. According to Citibank, the US is the top destination for foreign direct investment in the world; much of this money is used to build factories, which create jobs.[11]

All these transactions are lumped together in the capital and financial accounts. Since the balance of payments must balance (by definition), a deficit on the current account must be offset by a surplus on the capital and financial accounts.

It is easy to assume that it is the trade in goods and services that drives this relationship. But that's not necessarily the case. Many economists think that the capital account is the driving force. To understand this, imagine an island economy that is cut off from the rest of the world and doesn't have a government. People in that economy can either spend their money on goods and services or save it. The same goes for businesses; they can spend all the revenue they receive on wages and raw materials or they can save it. If they want to invest to expand production, they must use the money they saved, or borrow it from citizens (i.e. use the people's savings). In aggregate, they can only invest as much as the island saves.

Once a country starts trading with other nations, that restriction no longer applies. It can borrow money from abroad. In other words, if domestic savings are insufficient to fund desired domestic investment, then the country can import savings from abroad. This shows up as a surplus on the capital and financial accounts.

This explanation seems a perfect fit for the US. Its consumers tend to save less than those of many other countries. But its businesses, particularly in the technology sector, have ambitious investment plans. And its government regularly runs a big budget deficit. So, the US imports savings from abroad to finance these needs. And overseas savers are happy to oblige.

This savings/investment relationship has important implications for government policy. Three sectors save (or borrow): individuals, businesses and the government. The US government is a huge borrower, with a deficit reaching $1.8tn in 2024.[12] Republicans have proposed (at the time of writing) a further $4.6tn of tax cuts, offset by only $1.6tn of spending reductions.[13] Unless consumers and businesses start saving a lot more, this bigger budget deficit will make the trade deficit even bigger, the opposite of Mr Trump's stated desire of eliminating it.

The quickest way to cut a trade deficit is for consumers and businesses to stop spending, and save more. That would be an enormous hit to demand, which is why trade deficits normally fall in a recession. But such a cure is worse than the disease. In the longer term, the best way of bringing down the US trade deficit is to reduce the budget deficit. Since cutting taxes has repeatedly failed to do this, and since so much government spending goes to vital programmes such as Social Security, Medicare and defence, the obvious answer would be to increase taxes. But the Republicans, which have the backing of wealthy donors, dismiss this option.

Some economists take the contrary position and argue that the savings imbalance is driven by the export/import relationship. China saves so much and consumes so little that it generates a huge current account surplus that must be offset by deficits elsewhere in the world (in aggregate, the balance of payments of the world's nations must balance).[14] The US, as the world's largest economy, inevitably bears a lot of the burden of accommodating the Chinese surplus, such economists believe. But even if this is the case, a trade policy that affects the whole world, not just China, is the wrong way to tackle it.

In olden days, when trade deficits mattered

During the era of fixed exchange rates, trade deficits mattered a lot, because countries had to maintain the value of their currencies against gold or the US dollar. That required a nation's central bank to have some firepower in the form of foreign exchange reserves. When the currency came under pressure, the central bank could sell foreign currencies and buy its own to prop up the price. Accumulating foreign exchange reserves tended to require the country to run a trade surplus.

Persistent trade deficits might cause international investors to lose confidence in the exchange rate peg. To defend their currencies, central banks could, as well as using their reserves, push up interest rates. Higher rates would persuade investors to buy the currency. But higher rates would also slow the economy since consumers would have less money to buy imports. Sometimes, the required increase in rates was so large, and economically damaging, that governments decided to give up defending the currency, as happened when Britain dropped out of the European Exchange Rate Mechanism in 1992.

In today's world of mainly floating exchange rates, the trade deficit becomes much less important. If a nation's trade deficit is large, then it is possible for the country's currency to fall so that its exports are cheaper, and thus more attractive, and imports are more expensive, and thus less appealing. The trade deficit can right itself.

Some people argue that this mechanism fails to work in the case of the US because of the dollar's role as a global reserve currency. International demand for the dollar keeps its value high and thus prevents the trade deficit from correcting. The dollar has certainly strengthened since the financial crisis of 2007–9 but it is weaker than it was in 2000 or in the mid-1980s. It is also worth noting that the appeal of the dollar makes it easier to fund the US government's budget deficit and this may save taxpayers money in the form of reduced interest costs (this has been dubbed the US's 'exorbitant privilege').

When economists (and indeed most citizens) look at the main indicators of an economy's well-being, the trade position is nowhere near the top of the list. Is the economy growing? Are prices rising? Are jobs plentiful? These issues are much more important. Russia had a current account surplus in 2024 but it also had an inflation rate of 9.5 per cent and a GDP per capita only a sixth of the size of the US's. Dani Rodrik, a prominent economist who has been a critic of globalisation, said that there was 'absolutely no relationship between a country's trade deficit and how well it's doing'.[15]

So it is bizarre that the Trump administration has made trade such a prominent economic (or political) issue. And the next chapter will show why his chosen solution, tariffs, will make everything worse.

3

A TAX ON EFFICIENCY

'Those workmen, however, who suffered by our
neighbour's prohibition will not be benefited by ours.
On the contrary, they and almost all the other classes
of our citizens will thereby be obliged to pay dearer
than before for certain goods. Every such law, therefore,
imposes a real tax upon the whole country.'

Adam Smith, writing about retaliatory tariffs in
The Wealth of Nations

'We learned that a prohibitive protective tariff is a gun
that recoils upon ourselves.'

Cordell Hull, US secretary of state from 1933 to 1944

Tariffs have been a consistent tool of economic policy over
the centuries. In medieval Europe, local landlords built
castles on the Rhine to charge tolls (a kind of tariff) on
boats that passed by. This lucrative business caused the
lords to become known as 'robber barons' and the effect
was to discourage trade by making it too expensive. These

tolls weren't fully abolished until the nineteenth century.[1]

Adam Smith, generally regarded as the father of economics, opposed tariffs and the arguments he made still resonate today. He argued that tariffs interfere with the process of specialisation, preventing business from flowing to the most efficient producers. As a result, inefficient firms were allowed to stay afloat, holding back economic progress and forcing consumers to pay higher prices for inferior goods.

Often, tariffs are imposed at the insistence of one sector of the economy, at the expense of another. The *Economist* newspaper was founded in 1843 as part of a campaign to abolish the Corn Laws, a tax on imported grain. These laws favoured the agricultural elite that had long dominated British society but were opposed by factory owners, whose workers had to pay higher prices for food. In the US, during the nineteenth century, the political division was reversed. It was Northern industrialists who favoured tariffs to keep out British goods while Southern farmers wanted easy international access for their tobacco and cotton.

During the first great era of globalisation, from 1870 to 1914, many countries had tariffs to protect local industries but their impact was heavily diluted by the introduction of steamships and railways, which slashed the cost of transporting goods. The cost of shipping a bushel of grain between Chicago and Liverpool fell by two-thirds between the late 1850s and 1912.[2]

Protectionism returned in the interwar period. In 1930, Congress passed the Smoot–Hawley tariffs despite a letter from 1,028 economists in *The New York Times* denouncing the idea. The bill contained such absurd provisions as requiring all bottle corks to be stamped with their country of origin, a process that cost more than the making of the product itself.[3] Other countries retaliated and their imports from the US fell by around 30 per cent.[4] The impact of the Smoot–Hawley act was swallowed up by the calamity of the Great Depression which saw world trade fall by between a third and a half between 1930 and 1932. But the repair work started under President Franklin D. Roosevelt who pushed through the Reciprocal Trade Agreements Act of 1934, allowing him to negotiate lower rates with other nations.[5]

After 1945, democratic nations slowly dismantled trade barriers, including tariffs. Average tariff levels were around 22 per cent in 1947 when the General Agreement on Tariffs and Trade was set up.[6] They dropped to around 14 per cent by the mid-1960s. In 2000, the average tariff calculated by the WTO was 10.9 per cent and this fell further to 7.4 per cent in 2021; when tariff rates are weighted by the volume of trade, the levels were even lower, at 4.8 per cent in 2000 and 2.5 per cent in 2021.[7]

Taxing imports, bigly

If Donald Trump has any core belief, it is in tariffs. Back in 1989, when he was just a property developer, he told Diane Sawyer, a TV interviewer, that 'I believe very strongly in tariffs.' He added that 'America is being ripped off. We're a debtor nation, and we have to tax, we have to tariff, we have to protect this country.'[8] Over the intervening years, as Talleyrand remarked of the French Bourbon dynasty, he has 'learned nothing and forgotten nothing'.

At times, Mr Trump seems to treat tariffs as a 'miracle

cure' that can solve every ailment. Take his announcement, in May 2025, that he was planning to put 100 per cent tariffs on foreign-made films to save Hollywood from decline. The US film business has indeed been suffering but that is down to well-known factors such as the pandemic (which stopped cinema showings) and the rise of streaming services that allows people to view films at home. The idea that Hollywood has been undermined by foreign films, such as the South Korean Oscar-winner *Parasite*, is ridiculous.

Yes, some foreign countries (including Britain) have lured filmmakers overseas with tax breaks. But the film companies have used these facilities because they are cheaper. Making them move production back to the US will only increase their costs, worsening Hollywood's financial position, not improving it.

The problem with tariffs is that they are an incredibly blunt instrument that take no account of the complexities of individual industries. By levying a tariff, the government tries to impose its choice on where goods should be bought, with the result that consumers and businesses have to pay for inferior or more expensive goods. This is inevitably the case where there is no domestic equivalent (coffee beans, for example).

Historically, tariffs were usually levied on very discrete goods, such as wheat, alcohol and tea. But the Trump tariffs are being imposed not just on finished products but on the components as well. The administration talks of US cars, Canadian cars or European cars. Such a description is way too simplistic. Cars are not made in one place; they are assembled with components that come from all over the world. When Mexico exports cars to the US, for example, around three-quarters of the components were originally made in the US.[9] A tariff on Mexican cars is thus a tax on US component producers.

We are back to specialisation again. A manufacturer will want the most cost-efficient components to keep the price down. So, a tariff increases the costs of domestic producers. A Federal Reserve Bank of San Francisco survey in 2019 found that around 45 per cent of US-produced goods and services consisted of imports – components and raw materials brought in from overseas.[10] Under the Trump scheme, manufacturers will have to pay taxes on these inputs.

The Trump team has not grasped the way that the global economy is interconnected. The corporate sector developed its current structure in a world where tariffs were relatively low by historical standards, and there were no enormous barriers to moving goods back and forth across borders. This led companies to create complex supply chains, with components produced in many different nations, before being assembled elsewhere. Tariffs, and particularly tit-for-tat tariffs, make this model impossible to operate.

Perhaps the best illustration of the negative consequences of Mr Trump's tariff policies came in the form of a letter sent by the Footwear Distributors and Retailers of America (FDRA) to the president on 29 April.[11] 'American footwear businesses and families face an existential threat from such substantial cost increases,' the letter warned. 'Hundreds of businesses face the prospect of closure. Tens of thousands of jobs are at stake. Many orders have been placed on hold, and footwear inventory for US consumers may soon run low.'

The letter pointed out that the new tariffs piled up on existing ones, leading to overall rates ranging from 150 per cent to nearly 220 per cent (this was before the retreat on Chinese tariffs). These costs could not be absorbed or passed on to consumers, who are used to paying $30 to $50 for shoes. And the industry added that the existing tariffs had failed to stop domestic shoe production from declining. Furthermore, it would take years of planning and huge amounts of capital to shift sourcing back to the US. Even if the industry wanted to make this adjustment, the letter also pointed out that 'there is also a reciprocal tariff on the machinery and materials needed to make footwear in the US'.

Another problem with tariffs is that countries tend to retaliate. This is particularly the case with China, which matched Mr Trump's moves, step for step, in April. One reason why American farmers dug themselves out of the downturn they faced in the 1980s was that they were able to find export markets for their goods, with China a top target.

April Hemmes is an Iowa farmer who, as a member of the United Soybean Board, helped build the market for soybeans in China. She told *The New York Times*'s 'Daily' podcast in April 2025 that the Chinese take more than half of all US soybean exports and turn the bulk of it into meal for feeding pigs and chickens while the rest is used as oil for cooking.[12] Her business was hit by the trade dispute between the US and China in Mr Trump's first term and what bothered her about the current dispute was the lack of clarity about the future. 'In order to plan, we need certainty,' she said. Tariffs will cause her costs, in terms of seeds, chemicals and fertilisers, to rise while if China stops buying soybeans, the price of her crop will go down. She hoped that a deal could be arranged. 'Whether we like it or the president likes it, our economies need each other,' she said.

Fairness in trade

In his 2 April announcement, President Trump talked of reciprocity in trading arrangements. 'Reciprocal: that means they do it to us and we do it to them. Very simple, can't get any more simple than that,' he said.[13] So what have other countries actually been doing? In 1991, the average tariff rate imposed by low- and middle-income countries was nearly 33 per cent; for high-income countries, it was 9.2 per cent. By 2015, these rates were 8.2 per cent and 4.2 per cent respectively.[14]

In 2024, the average tariff rate of some of the US's main trading partners ranged from 1.7 per cent in Switzerland through 2.7 per cent in the European Union to 3 per cent in China; even in India, one of the more protectionist countries, they were 12 per cent.[15] In short, tariff rates have been falling, not rising, over time.

So do tariffs drive the trade deficit? In 1991, when tariff rates were much higher, the US recorded a current account surplus of 0.7 per cent of GDP.[16] The trade deficit was at its highest, as a percentage of GDP, in 2006 after global tariffs had been falling consistently for fifteen years.[17,18] In short, there is no relationship.

A World Bank study found that tariffs had only small effects on the trade balance. Indeed, it concluded that 'to the degree that tariffs are being deployed to achieve macroeconomic objectives (boost output, jobs, and the trade balance)' then such a policy 'will fail miserably to achieve its goal'.[19]

What tariffs have actually done

It is not necessary to speculate about the impact of tariffs, since it is possible to look at the historical experience of their effects. As mentioned in the Introduction, a paper by Davide Furceri of the International Monetary Fund (IMF) and others examined data from 151 countries in the period between 1963 and 2014 and found that tariffs had a statistically significant adverse impact on economic growth.[20] An increase of 3.6 percentage points in the tariff rate reduced growth by around 0.4 per cent over five years. That may not seem a lot but the combined effect of the initial set of Mr Trump's tariffs was to push up the average tariff (based on the proportion of trade with each country in 2024) by 25.6 percentage points to 28 per cent, the highest level since 1901.[21] (Even after the provisional deal with China, the effective tariff increase is around 15 percentage points – still a lot.)

The IMF academics found that the reduction in GDP growth came from several factors. First, labour is used less efficiently since it is diverted from efficient companies (which have to compete in the global market) to less efficient companies (which are sheltered by the tariffs from foreign competition). Second, tariffs tend to push up a country's exchange rate making exports less competitive. Third, since multinationals import many components, tariffs increase the costs of production. Finally, economic activity may speed up before the tariffs are imposed (as companies try to beat the tax) only to fall back again later.

In 2018, the first Trump administration imposed tariffs, first on washing machines and solar panels, and then on steel and aluminium. Later in the year, the US imposed a broad tariff on products from China of 10 per cent, increasing the rate to 25 per cent in 2019. China retaliated, as did the EU in respect of the steel and aluminium levies. Trading partners focused particularly on American agricultural products, such as the soybeans farmed by April Hemmes. As a result, the Trump administration was forced to institute a compensation programme for US farmers, which paid out $61bn over the course of 2018 to 2020, eating up nearly all the income generated by the tariffs.[22]

Why was Trump's plan such a bust? A paper from the National Bureau of Economic Research found that importers who had previously bought from China didn't switch to suppliers at home but just bought their goods from other countries.[23] Another problem was the tariffs on items such as steel and aluminium increased the costs of domestic manufacturers, making their products more expensive (and thus less competitive). The value of sales went up but not the number of units or the number of employees needed to make those units.

But think of the money

Tariffs are taxes. President Trump has talked about creating an 'external revenue service' to collect all the taxes that will, he says, be paid by foreigners. In practice, however, tariffs are paid by the importer when the goods enter the country. That is why General Motors talked of suffering a tariff cost of $4–5bn.

But where will the burden of these extra costs actually fall? This is what economists call the 'incidence' of tariffs. There are several options. First, the cost can be passed directly on to consumers. Second, the importing company can absorb the cost itself, by reducing its profit margin. And third, the importer can go back to the exporting company and ask it to lower its price so that its cost, after the tariff, is unchanged. Or some combination of the three could occur.

How the incidence will fall depends on a range of factors, from the type of goods concerned to how dependent the exporters are on the US for their sales. If the US is blocked, Chinese suppliers can try to sell their goods in the EU or other developing nations, which have yet to respond to Mr Trump's actions by imposing their own extra tariffs on overseas goods. As for the clothing suppliers in places like Vietnam or Bangladesh, their room for adjustment is very limited. They already pay low wages and the idea that they could cut prices to absorb the kind of tariffs imposed in the 2 April package is clearly absurd. That means the burden will fall on importers and their customers.

How much will the Trump tax raise?

Whoever pays the Trump tariffs, they will undoubtedly raise revenue for the US government. But will that be enough to transform the government's finances? One chart that circulated in 2025 showed the period in the late nineteenth century when tariffs funded much of government spending. The chart was tweeted by Marc Andreessen, a venture capitalist, and sent by Donald Trump to his followers. Mr Trump is also fond of citing the example of William McKinley, a Republican president from 1897 to 1901, who was dubbed the 'tariff king'.

Back in 1900, however, federal spending was just 3 per

cent of GDP. There was no government programme to pay pensions, or unemployment benefits; no programmes like Medicare or Medicaid to provide healthcare for the elderly and the poor. Defence spending also increased dramatically during the two world wars and the Cold War that followed. In 1913, the US brought in a federal income tax and, later, a payroll tax to fund Social Security. These taxes raise a lot more revenue than tariffs ever did, and they fund a much bigger state than was ever envisaged in 1900.[24]

Mr Trump has suggested that tariffs might replace income tax for those earning less than $200,000. This is just not plausible. The federal government raised $2.4tn from income taxes on individuals in 2024;[25] tariff income is likely to generate only a fraction of this number. The Tax Policy Center estimates that the tariffs, as adjusted after the 9 April retreat, will raise around $170bn a year.[26]

Indeed, how could the US replace the $2.4tn brought in by income tax given the actual level of trade? The US imported $4.1tn worth of goods and services in 2024, of which $3.3tn was goods.[27] High tariff rates will surely reduce that amount, particularly in the case of the levies imposed on China, which exported $439bn worth of goods to the US in 2024.[28] After all, the tariffs cannot both raise a lot of money, and simultaneously be successful in reducing imports or in bringing production back to the US.

Tariffs and influence

Tariffs have such an adverse impact on businesses that companies will be encouraged to lobby the government to dilute their impact. In late April, Javier Selgas, the chief executive of Freight Technologies, a trucking firm, said it had bought $20m worth of a Trump memecoin as 'an effective way to advocate for fair, balanced and free trade between Mexico and the US'.[29] Trucking companies are likely to take a big hit when the trade dries up, as they transport goods from ports and other entry points to distribution centres around the US.

That a Trump memecoin exists at all is a sign that financial and ethical standards are much less stringent under the current presidency. The coin was launched in January 2025, with 1 billion coins created; 800 million of these were reserved for Trump owned companies. Like many other cryptocurrencies, the coin has no asset backing. But it is natural for some investors to assume that buying the coin would curry favour with, or give them access to, the president. Sure enough, the top 220 holders of the coin were invited to a private dinner with Mr Trump in May.[30] To put this into context, the Whitewater scandal, which dominated the media headlines during the Clinton Presidency (1993–2001), revolved around a failed investment of $203,000 and a $300,000 loan.[31] In contrast, the *Financial Times* estimated that Trump companies earned $350m from the memecoin.[32]

As his 'kissing my ass' comments demonstrated, one of the reasons President Trump likes tariffs is that they force other national leaders to approach him as supplicants. Corporate executives and foreign politicians alike have to pay court, as if he were a medieval monarch.

The president's power is all the greater because of the way that these latest tariffs are being imposed. Under the US Constitution Article 1, Section 8, 'The Congress shall have power to lay and collect taxes, duties, imposts and excises.'[33] But President Trump is bypassing this control by invoking the International Emergency Economic Powers Act which allows the president to regulate imports during a 'national emergency'.[34]

To which the obvious retort is, what emergency? US GDP grew by a real rate of 2.8 per cent in 2024,[35] making the economy 12.1 per cent larger than before the pandemic, an improvement far above that achieved by any other G7 country.[36] The US inflation rate was 2.9 per cent and falling at the end of 2024.[37] An earlier bout of inflation was blamed by some voters on President Biden, but while his fiscal stimulus had some effect, the main culprits were pandemic shortages and Russia's invasion of Ukraine, which caused prices to rise across the developed world. American wage growth outstripped inflation in 2024, meaning that real wages grew by 1.2 per cent, an improvement in the standard of living. The US unemployment rate was 4.1 per cent in December 2024, a modest level given that unemployment had been above 5 per cent for a substantial chunk of the post-1945 period.[38]

So well has the US economy been performing, in relative terms, that the *Economist* published a special report in October 2024 calling it the 'envy of the world' and noting that 'in the history of modern economics America's three-decade outperformance is remarkable'.[39] As for citing the trade deficit as an 'emergency', the gap between imports and exports, as a proportion of GDP, has been steady in recent years and is lower than it was twenty years ago.[40]

That the 'emergency' argument was a stretch was demonstrated in late May when the US Court of International

Trade ruled that the president had exceeded his powers by imposing a broad range of tariffs (although not the levies on specific sectors such as steel and cars, which are based on the need to protect national security). This will undoubtedly lead to a court battle and may prompt Mr Trump to use other rules (like the ones which allowed him to tax steel imports) to get his way.

Of course, the reason that President Trump wanted to use the emergency rule was to bypass Congress and avoid any checks on his actions. A really determined Congress could have challenged him, but the Republicans have proved supine. That the party nominated Mr Trump for president in 2024 is salutary, given the storming of the Capitol in January 2021. But those few who stood up to him in 2021 lost their seats, as the president's loyal base of voters rallied against them in primary campaigns. All future resistance was crushed and there is little hope of finding principled opposition now.

Giving all this economic power to Mr Trump is dangerous since he has already shown that he cares little for the ethical rules that have constrained most presidents. The link between tariffs and corruption has been well demonstrated elsewhere. When companies need to import materials or components, they attempt to get tariffs reduced. A paper for the *American Economic Review* in 2016 found that, in southern Africa, pervasive corruption meant that 'even small bribes can significantly reduce tariffs'.[41]

Alternatively, domestic producers can lobby to keep tariffs high to exclude foreign competition. An analysis of the impact of tariffs in Latin America found that, over time, businesses shifted their focus from 'improving productivity to lobbying for favorable treatment'. Inefficient companies thrived because of their political connections, even though their factories were well behind the standards prevailing in the global market.[42] Since the global market was shut out by the tariffs, this didn't matter.

One final point is worth making about tariffs, given the rhetoric that has come from the Republican Party over the last forty years about free markets, and their resistance to some measures such as increasing the federal minimum wage. Tariffs are a massive interference with free markets. Of course, markets do not always work perfectly. They are, for example, bad at dealing with externalities, the term economists use to describe the indirect benefits or costs of a transaction (such as pollution) that may affect others.

But economists generally accept that the variability of prices is very useful. Rising prices send signals to producers to increase production; falling prices send a signal to reduce production or cut costs. Tariffs clearly interfere with these signals since they are sent not by the market, but by the government. Higher tariffs on steel or cars are not a sign that consumer demand for these products is soaring. To the extent that they prompt domestic companies to change their plans, tariffs may be diverting firms from producing goods that are actually in greater demand. Instead they will focus on areas where they are less efficient but have protection from foreign competition.

Even if Mr Trump's supporters accept that tariffs are a crude instrument, they argue that they are needed to tackle the big problem: the loss of manufacturing jobs. What has caused that decline is the subject of the next chapter.

4

WHERE THE JOBS WENT

'A manufacturing nation is, in every sense of the word, dependent on others.'

John Tyler, US President (1841–5)

If there is an over-riding rationale behind the Trump tariffs, it is a desire to bring manufacturing jobs back to the US. Manufacturing's share of total US non-farm employment fell from 32 per cent in 1950 to just 8 per cent in 2024.[1] When assigning the blame for those lost jobs, many Americans today point the finger at China. But China didn't join the World Trade Organization until 2001, the point at which its industries got greater access to western markets. By that stage, the share of manufacturing employment as a percentage of the US total had already fallen by 20 percentage points to just 12 per cent.[2]

There was undoubtedly a 'China shock' in the first decade of the twenty-first century which cost millions of jobs in the US and, according to one influential paper from the National Bureau of Economic Research, had severe

impacts in some regions with 'wages and labor-force partici-
pation rates remaining depressed and unemployment rates
remaining elevated for at least a full decade'.[3]

But the actions of foreign countries can't be the only
culprit behind the jobs decline. For a start, trade is a much
smaller proportion of US GDP than it is for other advanced
economies like Germany, France and the UK.[4] The US trade
deficit in goods is only around 4 per cent of GDP. Even
if that was entirely eliminated and replaced by domestic
production, this would only make a small addition to the
manufacturing sector's share of the economy, perhaps 2.5
percentage points, reckons the economist Paul Krugman.[5]
(Not 4 points because manufacturers spend a lot on services
like accounting, marketing and software.)

Furthermore, the fall in manufacturing jobs was observ-
able in all the G7 economies. Whether they had a trade
surplus (Germany) or a deficit (the UK), the pace of decline
was steady. Even in the period 1990 to 2003, a pretty good
era for economic growth, manufacturing employment in
the average OECD nation declined by nearly 10 percentage
points.[6]

Will tariffs help to restore those jobs? Not if the experience of the first Trump administration is any guide. A paper
from the National Bureau of Economic Research that examined the impact of the 2018 and 2019 tariffs found that they
had 'neither a sizable nor significant effect on US employment' in regions with a large concentration in the industries
Trump protected.[7] An even gloomier conclusion was
reached by a Federal Reserve study in 2019 which looked at
the tariffs and found that they were associated with relative

reductions in manufacturing employment. 'Rising input costs and retaliatory tariffs each contribute to the negative relationship, and the contribution from these channels more than offsets a small positive effect from import protection,' the authors found.[8]

Meanwhile, a study by CESifo, a German think tank, found that the first wave of Trump tariffs did create jobs – *but in Brazil*. Since the US and China imposed tariffs on each other, companies looked to source their goods from third countries. The study found that employment rose much more in Brazilian regions that specialised in the products (mainly steel and aluminium) that were subject to retaliatory tariffs than in regions which did not produce such goods.[9]

But the story of lost manufacturing jobs does not mean that manufacturing output has been in relentless decline. Over the past thirty years, output has grown around 30 per cent in real terms.[10] The sector has seen significant improvements in productivity, particularly in areas such as electronics and computers. In terms of the latter, the gains have been exponential: the computing power of your smartphone is significantly greater than that of 'supercomputers' developed in the 1980s.[11]

Increasing productivity means producing more items with fewer inputs and one of those inputs is labour. This has been the most important factor in the decline in manufacturing jobs. A paper by Michael Hicks and Srikant Devaraj found that almost 88 per cent of the jobs lost in the first decade of the twenty-first century were the result of productivity gains, rather than trade.[12]

Those productivity improvements have allowed US manufacturers to move up the value chain, making goods that require more expertise, such as aerospace, and avoiding lower-margin activities, such as textiles. As a result, the value added per US worker has doubled since 1990 and is the highest in the world, many times that of China.[13]

The modern economy is a service economy

The corollary is that, as manufacturing declined, the service sector rose. Its share of value added in the US economy jumped from 52 per cent in 1950 to 79 per cent in 2020, while services now comprise 85 per cent of all employment and 78 per cent of all household spending.[14] This is a trend that is common across all advanced economies.

In 1950, US consumers spent 60 per cent of their income on goods. Now the proportion is just a third with services taking up the slack.[15] Activities such as going on holiday, eating at a restaurant, or watching the latest show on a streaming service are increasingly popular. As far back as 1998, an article in *Harvard Business Review* talked of the 'experience economy' in which companies competed to create memorable events.[16] The rise of social media, where consumers post pictures of themselves eating a meal or sightseeing, has exacerbated the trend.

Something similar happened in the nineteenth century when there was a huge shift in employment from agriculture to manufacturing. Nowadays, the developed world can feed itself even though only 1–2 per cent of its population works in agriculture. Modern farms are much more productive than their Victorian-era equivalents.

Given that the current economy is service-dominated, the logical focus of anyone concerned with the health of the US economy should be on services, in which the country has a trade surplus. By pushing through tariffs, and disrupting the flow of trade, Mr Trump is damaging the biggest section of the economy (through the hit to both business and consumer confidence) to (attempt to) benefit a much smaller element.

In the view of some critics, however, service-sector jobs are not as good as those in manufacturing. They point to areas such as warehouses or delivery driving, where workers are on low wages and zero-hour contracts, in what is dubbed the 'precariat'. But while there was some evidence for the growth of low-skilled jobs in the first decade of the twenty-first century, when the China shock was greatest, a recent paper found this effect has disappeared. Between 2016 and 2022, there were declines in low-skilled and middle-skilled US jobs. At the same time there was rapid growth in high-paying jobs. Specifically, jobs linked to science, technology, engineering and maths have grown from 6.5 per cent of the US workforce in 2010 to 10 per cent. American skills are being upgraded, the authors conclude.[17]

It is also unwise to paint too rosy a picture of what it is like to hold a manufacturing job. A study by Anne Case and Angus Deaton, two of the most influential researchers in the field, found that those involved in manual labour report both worse, and more rapidly deteriorating, health than those in other occupations, even when controlling for income and education.[18] And a long-term study of Danish workers found that physically demanding jobs were linked to shorter working lives, more sick leave and more unemployment.[19]

When Detroit ruled the auto sector

The desire to rely on domestic, rather than foreign, suppliers raises more complex issues, as the history of the car industry demonstrates. When it comes to nostalgia about the heyday of manufacturing labour, jobs in the car industry are one of the most-cited examples. Until the 1970s, nearly nine out of ten of all cars made in the US were produced by one of the 'big three' – General Motors, Ford and Chrysler. The cars they made were often large and had very poor mileage per gallon, but in those days gasoline was cheap.

Work for the big three companies was well-paid with good holidays and pension rights. That was in large part due to the power of the United Auto Workers union. As an example, in 1970, it staged a sixty-seven-day nationwide strike at General Motors which resulted in the union winning a $20 per week pay rise (about 12 per cent) and the right to retire at fifty-eight, after thirty years of service.[20,21]

In 1973, however, the OPEC oil embargo forced up the price of gasoline. Suddenly, US drivers became interested in smaller cars which consumed less fuel. The big three were slow to adapt to the new conditions and stuck with high labour costs. They lost market share to more nimble Japanese manufacturers such as Toyota and Honda, the start of their long, slow decline.

The shrinking was most notable in Detroit, known as the 'Motor City' for its focus on car production (the Motown record label was a contraction of 'motor town').

Its population fell by 61 per cent between 1950 and 2010 as car jobs disappeared.[22] Foreign car makers that set up factories in the US went to the Southern states, which have anti-union rules; by 2023, the South was home to 30 per cent of all US car jobs.[23] The incoming manufacturers clearly decided that they could not make money operating in the same way as the big three companies.

As a result, US car manufacturing jobs are not the money-spinners that they used to be. Economist Paul Krugman pointed out that workers at McDonald's restaurants in Denmark are currently paid $20 an hour (plus benefits) while production associates at the Honda plant in Alabama are paid just $14 an hour.[24] Bringing back car jobs to the US will not bring back 1950s-style prosperity for blue-collar workers.

Back then, industries of all kinds had unions to protect them, and Trump's nostalgia only extends so far. Although Mr Trump received support from a significant minority (around 45 per cent) of union members, his record has been generally anti-union, ripping up labour contracts with federal workers and dismissing the head of the National Labor Relations Board, which protects the rights of private-sector employees.[25]

Weaker unions are one potential reason why employees have lost the power to demand higher wages. The proportion of US workers who are in a union was 9.9 per cent in 2024, down from 20.1 per cent in 1983, according to the Bureau of Labor Statistics.[26] Many of those members are in the public sector; the proportion of private-sector workers who are in a union is just 5.9 per cent, down from around one in three in the 1950s.[27] Unionised workers are better paid, earning an average $1,337 per week, compared with just $1,137 for their non-unionised counterparts (some of this may be down to occupational differences).[28]

The problems with reshoring

When it comes to low-skilled employment, US manufacturers have a problem: it costs a lot more to make things in the US. Motorola discovered this when it opened a smartphone factory in Fort Worth, Texas, in 2013. Sadly, it closed twelve months later because of high costs.[29] And that is hardly surprising since the average pay of a US manufacturing worker is twice that of their Chinese equivalent and six times that of Vietnam.[30]

Over time, the biggest job losses in US manufacturing occurred in sectors such as textiles or metals, where the lower costs of producers in Asia made it hard for western companies to compete. But employment actually grew in pharmaceuticals, a higher-margin business where the greater skills and productivity of US workers gave them an advantage.

Adam Smith would have recognised the trend. The US has specialised in those parts of the manufacturing sector where it has advantages – a skilled workforce and ready access to capital. The result has been a focus on products with higher profit margins and a shift away from goods where fewer skills are needed and profit margins are low.

Bringing back manufacturing jobs will also cost money. It requires at least $25m, and takes around two years, to build a simple, mid-sized factory, according to an estimate by Andreas Haag of Streamliners, a consultancy. More complex projects will cost a lot more.[31] Dan Ives, an analyst at the financial group Wedbush, estimated that Apple would need three years and $30bn to move just 10 per cent of its supply chain from Asia to the US.[32] Indeed, Apple's immediate response to the tariff package was to shift production from China to India, not the US.[33] This news generated a tariff threat from Mr Trump, but it would need very high levies to offset the additional costs of US-based manufacturing.

The rising cost of building factories is in part due to planning delays, objections from local residents and a shortage of labour in construction.[34] Tariffs on steel and other products will add substantially to that bill.

Haas Automation is a company that makes high-end industrial machinery. Peter Zierhut, the company's vice president, told the *Wall Street Journal* that it was unrealistic to expect US suppliers to establish factories to make basic, low-margin products, like the 100 million pounds of cast iron it imports from China. Mr Zierhut said that building a new foundry would require hundreds of millions of dollars of investment to create a product that sells for a few dollars a pound. The company added that it had already cut production and eliminated overtime at its California plant and might delay the opening of a plant in Nevada. That is because the cost of imported iron would force it to increase its prices.[35]

Given the time taken to build new factories, it will be hard to reshore many products. Manufacturers interviewed by the *Wall Street Journal* said that it was very tough to find domestic suppliers for some key components, as the businesses were either non-existent, produced in insufficient quantities, or charged prices that were too high.[36] One company, Rapid Plastics, which makes coat hangers for department stores, said that all the domestic suppliers of metal hooks had closed or gone abroad.

And why should businesses shift production when they can't be sure how long the latest Trump tariff package will last? This uncertainty is one of the biggest negative consequences of Mr Trump. A research note from Jefferies, an investment bank, published in April, said that 'The downside risk of investing in US plants without stable trade agreements is substantial, potentially deterring companies from establishing their manufacturing operations. This uncertainty can lead to hesitancy in making long-term investments, impacting the growth and stability of the US manufacturing sector.'

A further problem is that the US already has a shortage of manufacturing workers. Around 20 per cent of manufacturing plants in 2024 said that a lack of labour prevented them from operating at full capacity.[37] The challenge was even more acute in textiles, where nearly 28 per cent of plants reported a labour shortfall; clothing is one of the sectors most exposed to price increases from Trump's original tariff package, thanks to the amount of production in low-wage Asia. If companies can't recruit enough textile workers now, how will they manage if they try to replace suppliers in Vietnam or Bangladesh?

Recruitment is hard because factory jobs aren't deemed to be appealing. A poll by the Cato Institute found that, while 80 per cent of Americans thought that the country would be better off if more of its citizens worked in a factory, only around a quarter thought they personally would be better off with such a job.[38]

To the extent that manufacturers have been able to fill vacancies, it has been by attracting workers from abroad. A paper from the Federal Reserve Bank of Kansas City found that 2.5 million immigrant workers joined the labour force in 2022 and a further 1.5 million did so in 2023. This helped alleviate the staffing shortages that had emerged during the pandemic. It also helped to cool inflationary pressures.[39] Mr Trump's actions in clamping down on immigration, and his hostility towards overseas citizens already living in the country, will eliminate this source of additional labour.

To which, some critics may say 'good'. They want American jobs for American workers. The problem with this argument is what economists call the 'lump of labour fallacy', the idea that there is only a set amount of work to go round. The fallacy has been much cited in the past, to argue, for example, that women should keep out of the workforce so all the jobs can be reserved for men. But the history of the US shows that, despite a lot of immigration and a fast-rising population, there has always been a lot of work to go around. In February 2025, there were 159 million people in US non-farm employment, a new record, up from 30 million back in 1939 and 109 million in 1990.[40] Every new worker is also a source of demand; they spend money on goods and services that provide jobs for other workers.

Immigrant workers are also an important source of innovation. Immigrants are responsible for founding a fifth of all start-up companies that are financed by venture capital, and a quarter of all the 'unicorn' companies (unquoted businesses valued at more than $1bn) were founded by immigrants who arrived on a student visa.[41]

The current shortfall in the US labour force is likely to get worse, not better. A report by the consultancy Deloitte estimated that 3.8 million new manufacturing workers would be needed by 2033.[42] But only 1 million of those new hires would be the result of industry growth. The main problem would be the 2.8 million replacement workers needed as existing employees retired.

Deloitte's report worried that the industry would struggle to fill 1.9 million, or half, of those roles because of a shortage of applicants with the right skills. Attracting and retaining the right workers was seen as the main challenge by more than 65 per cent of respondents in a survey by the National Association of Manufacturers.[43] In short, if the US does want to expand the manufacturing sector, it cannot expect to just pull people off the street. At the very least, it will require extensive amounts of retraining. But in 2021, the US spent less on retraining than most advanced countries.[44]

Because of this worker shortage, shifting production to low-margin activities to avoid tariffs would require US companies to take resources away from their high-margin businesses. This makes no economic sense. It would be like a Michelin-starred restaurant charging $100 a meal suddenly shifting to offering burgers and fries at $9.99. That is one of the many reasons why tariffs hinder, rather than help, economic growth.

Given these factors, it is unsurprising that a survey of Texan manufacturers by the Federal Reserve Bank of Dallas found that 67 per cent thought that tariffs would have a negative impact on their business in 2025. Around four-fifths thought they would face higher input costs, and about two-thirds expected to have lower profit margins. Around 44 per cent expected to reduce their capital spending, compared with just 12 per cent who thought it would increase. More than a third thought they would decrease employment compared with just 1.4 per cent who expected the introduction of tariffs to increase recruitment.

As for the 'incidence' of tariffs, 76 per cent said they would pass through the cost to customers, more than any other option. More manufacturers (13 per cent) thought that they would scale down production or close their business than the 11 per cent who thought that they would relocate production to the US.[45]

Support, not block

Although the above analysis might seem a counsel of despair for US manufacturing jobs, there are things that can be done to improve the situation. One president did manage to increase the number of manufacturing jobs during his first term of office: Joe Biden. There was a net gain of 610,000 jobs from 12,145,000 in January 2021 to 12,755,000 in January 2025, when he left office.[46] Admittedly, Mr Biden took over during the pandemic, when employment was depressed. Nevertheless, manufacturing employment peaked at 12.9 million during his administration, the highest level since the financial crisis of 2007–9.[47]

While the Biden administration imposed some tariffs on Chinese goods, the main focus of his economic policy was on subsidies, particularly for the production of batteries, computer chips and green energy. The result was the announcement of a number of new factories, including an electric vehicle battery plant in Michigan and a solar manufacturing plant in Georgia.[48] In terms of semiconductors, which many see as a vital strategic industry, the programme attracted around $450bn in private-sector investment in US plants.[49]

But the problem for Mr Biden was that such investment takes a lot of time to reach fruition. The 2024 election was too early for voters to see the benefits since a lot of the factories were yet to be built. The above-mentioned Deloitte report calculated that nearly 300 clean technology and electronics manufacturing plants were scheduled to be built thanks to the various incentive plans introduced by the Biden administration. In total, these would have produced 234,000 new manufacturing jobs.[50]

Many of these planned jobs may now be at risk because the Trump administration has halted a wide range of projects related to renewable energy and electric car charging.[51] Mr Trump's dislike for renewable energy is simply irrational; the costs of solar energy have dropped by 90 per cent over the last ten years, while those of wind energy have fallen 70 per cent.[52] But rather than invest in the industries of the future, Mr Trump wants to turn back to the industries of the past, like coal and oil.

In the long run, the US should really be worried about the challenge from China, not in low-margin industries like assembling electronic products, but in new areas such as artificial intelligence. China's development of the Deep-Seek large language model came as a shock to American companies that had previously dominated the field.[53] It emerged despite, or perhaps because of, US attempts under both Presidents Trump and Biden to constrain China's technological development. The Royal United Services Institute, a defence think tank, argues that the sanctions may 'have been counterproductive, in the sense that they have galvanized an ecosystem of Chinese businesses to finally come on board with policy initiatives to indigenize high-end technology capabilities'.[54]

The US would do better to focus on ensuring its own scientists and technologists have all the resources they need. That is why picking fights, and taking away funds, from leading research universities like Harvard over issues such as antisemitism or 'woke' ideology is so foolish. China will be delighted if the US turns on its academics, and will be especially pleased if Chinese students carry on their work at home, rather than emigrate to the US.

The oil paradox

It is not just manufacturing where the Trump agenda faces serious practical problems. The president used the slogan 'drill, baby, drill' to emphasise his desire to push up domestic oil production and ignore objections from environmentalists. This increased production would drive down the price of gasoline, a sensitive topic for US consumers; high gasoline prices were a common complaint under the Biden administration.

The problem is that the US is sitting on top of the wrong type of oil. Much US production comes in the form of shale, an expensive and environmentally dubious resource

process that involves drilling into rock and using vast quantities of pressurised water. Industry insiders reckon that shale
producers need a price of at least $60, and probably $65 or
higher, a barrel to be profitable.[55] By early May 2025, the
crude oil price had dropped below $60 a barrel on fears that
the global economy would slow in the face of Mr Trump's
tariffs. Saudi Arabia, which has about the lowest oil production costs in the world, can make money at that price;[56] US
producers will struggle. As with the tariff policy, what might
be good for US producers is not good for US consumers, and
vice versa. And the effect on consumers is the subject of the
next chapter.

5

WHERE ALL PEOPLE ARE CREATED UNEQUAL

'Acting without thinking is like shooting without aiming.'

B. C. Forbes, journalist (1880–1954)

'We were losing hundreds of billions of dollars with China. Now we're essentially not doing business with China. Therefore, we're saving hundreds of billions of dollars. It's very simple'.

Donald Trump, interview with NBC News, 4 May 2025

Perhaps the most enduring aspect of Donald Trump's appeal to the electorate is the belief that he is fighting the corner of the working family. Many people who vote for him may not like his style, but they have been persuaded that he is a shrewd businessman who will do more for the average American than the typical Republican or Democratic politician.

Mr Trump pitches his trade policy in this light, claiming that it will bring prosperity for all Americans. 'These tariffs are going to give us growth like you've never seen before, and it'll be something very special to watch,' he said, when announcing his package on 2 April.[1] The problem, to adapt the Forbes quote that began this chapter, is that Mr Trump and his advisers have adopted a protectionist trade policy without thinking through the implications.

Tariffs are not the panacea that Mr Trump seems to think they are. And most Americans sense that. A Gallup poll in late April found that 62 per cent of Americans thought that tariffs would cost the US more money than they would generate in the long run (70 per cent also thought this was true of the short run).[2]

The last chapter argued that a trade war in general, and the tariffs in particular, would not generate a mass return of manufacturing jobs to the US. And Chapter 3 argued that the bulk of the burden of the tariffs would fall on US businesses and consumers. Again, the US public is wise to this. Nearly 90 per cent of those questioned in the Gallup poll thought that the tariffs were very or somewhat likely to result in higher prices.

This chapter will look more specifically at which citizens will be most affected by Mr Trump's broad range of policies. While Mr Trump has claimed that the tariffs are an 'external revenue service', a lot of the burden will fall on American consumers. That is clear from a May announcement by Walmart, the world's largest retailer. John David Rainey, the company's chief financial officer, said that 'We're wired for everyday low prices, but the magnitude of these increases is more than any retailer can absorb. It's more than any supplier can absorb. And so I'm concerned that [the] consumer is going to start seeing higher prices.'[3] Where Walmart leads, other companies are likely to follow.[4]

In mid-May, the Budget Lab at Yale University calculated that the Trump tariff package implied a 1.7 percentage point increase in inflation (had the full set of tariffs on China been maintained the effect would have been 3 percentage points). That was equivalent to a loss of purchasing power of $2,800 per household. Shoes would cost 15 per cent more and clothing 14 per cent more.[5] In the long run, companies may be able to switch away from Chinese suppliers but, for the moment, the US is extremely reliant on China for some categories of goods. Ninety per cent of microwaves and electric fans imported by the US in 2024 came from China, for example, along with 80 per cent of smartphones.[6] Finding alternative suppliers at short notice will be extremely difficult.

Affording these higher prices will be even harder because jobs will be less plentiful. Yale also estimated that the Trump tax would cause unemployment to rise by 0.4 percentage points and GDP growth to be 0.7 points lower in 2025 than it would otherwise have been.[7]

At the time of writing, the Tax Foundation, a non-partisan think tank, estimated that the tariffs would reduce after-tax income by an average of $1,183 per household in 2025, or 1.1 per cent.[8] Overall, the tariffs represent the largest tax increase on US citizens since 1993.

The impact of tariffs on prices is not the only burden on poorer Americans imposed by Mr Trump's economic programme. In his budget plan, sent to Congress in May, the president proposed the elimination of the Low Income Home Energy Assistance Program, which helps poorer consumers with their utility bills (the staff who run it had already been fired).[9] Another planned cut is to an educational programme that gives assistance to students from poorer backgrounds.[10] Proposals pushed forward by House Republicans would enforce cuts to affordable food programmes (now known as SNAP), Medicaid (health insurance for the poor) and Medicare (health insurance for the elderly).[11]

These cuts hardly point to an administration that is on the side of the common man against the 'elite'. Nor are these cuts part of a blueprint to balance the budget. Mr Trump also wants to extend the tax cuts passed in 2017, during his first term. The non-partisan Tax Policy Center reckons that extending the 2017 cuts would reduce federal revenues by an average of $460bn a year over the next ten years. Around two-thirds of the benefits of these tax reductions would go to the highest 20 per cent of US earners. The poorest 20 per cent of earners would receive an income boost of just 0.6 per cent a year.[12]

In May, after the Republicans in Congress unveiled their full budget proposal, the Center on Budget and Policy Priorities calculated that the tax cuts alone would deliver a 4.3 per cent increase in income for the wealthiest 1 per cent of Americans; in cash terms, that would be an average of $64,770. The poorest 20 per cent of the population would receive just a 0.6 per cent boost, or an average of $90. Of course, the wealthiest pay the most tax. Still, when you combine the tax cuts with the impact of the tariffs (a tax on consumption), the top 1 per cent would get a 3 per cent income boost, while the bottom 20 per cent would lose an average of 0.6 per cent.[13] That is because the rich save a big chunk of their income while the poor spend almost all of theirs (and thus pay proportionately more of the Trump tax).

These figures do not take account of the impact of cuts in Medicaid and SNAP which will fall exclusively on the poor. Initial estimates suggest that the cuts in the Medicaid programme would result in 10.3 million people losing medical coverage by 2034 and 7.6 million people going without health insurance.[14] Planned cuts to reduce funding for the SNAP programme, by passing more of the burden to the states, could remove food aid from a quarter of all recipients, many of whom live in the rural areas that voted for Mr Trump.[15] This is not standing up for the working family so much as stamping down on them.

Not all created equal

All these tax changes and spending cuts will only reinforce the unequal nature of the US economy. The Gini coefficient measures the distribution of income through an economy. A figure close to 1 means incomes are highly concentrated in the hands of a few people; a figure closer to 0 means greater equality. The average Gini coefficient across the OECD is 0.313, but the US is at 0.395. This may not seem like a big difference but it is significant. Every European country (for which the OECD has figures) is more equal than this level. Sweden and Norway are at 0.286 and 0.285 respectively.[16] This equality has not held back the Norwegian economy; thanks to its oil and gas resources, Norway is a wealthier country, in terms of GDP per capita, than the US.

In the average OECD country, the top 10 per cent of households own 51.7 per cent of the wealth. In Belgium and Japan, the ratio is 47.3 per cent; in France it is 49.2 per cent. In the US, the ratio is 79.1 per cent, a proportion that is more than 16 percentage points higher than that of any other nation for which the OECD gives figures.[17] These wealth disparities were not imposed by China or the EU; nor are they the inevitable consequences of globalisation, a phenomenon that every OECD nation faces. These inequalities are the result of decisions made by American politicians.

When US workers lose their jobs, their entitlement to benefits is worse than in any other OECD country bar Hungary, with which it is tied. After one year without employment, a single person without children receives 9 per cent of their previous pay in the US; in six European countries, the proportion is more than 70 per cent.[18]

The US is one of only two developed countries without a national mandate that workers should get sick pay (some individual states, such as California, do require this).[19] There is also no federally mandated minimum period of annual leave, nor indeed any federal requirement to grant maternity leave. Again, this is a political choice.

Some Republicans might argue that the absence of these provisions allows employers and employees more flexibility to negotiate in a free market. But it is odd that employers can choose on what terms they employ their workers, but not (thanks to tariffs) which suppliers they can use.

By and large, then, workers have fewer rights in the US than in other countries. In theory, this means the US labour market is more flexible and workers find it easier to get jobs.

And it is certainly true that, in 2024, the US's unemployment rate of 4.1 per cent was below the global average of 4.9 per cent.[20] But this labour market flexibility hasn't done a lot for manufacturing employment. In France, where labour rights are very strong, manufacturing jobs are 11 per cent of total employment;[21] in the US, just 8 per cent.

The UN produces a human development index which combines measures of national income, longevity and years spent in education. Although the US is often described as the richest nation in the world, it is not top of this table, but equal seventeenth (with Liechtenstein and New Zealand).[22] Many European nations are ahead of the US on the human development index, as are Australia, Canada, Hong Kong, Singapore and the United Arab Emirates. Strikingly, US life expectancy is four years below that of both Sweden and Singapore. Again, these figures are the result of domestic policies, not of those of trading partners.

What about the sluggishness of gains in living standards, which may underlie the discontent of Mr Trump's core voters? As John Lettieri[23] and Noah Smith[24] have pointed out, the longest period of stagnation in US real wages occurred between 1973 and 1995, before China's entry into the WTO. The US joined the North American Free Trade Agreement (NAFTA) in 1994, which some argued would be bad for US workers, but real wages actually rose sharply after 1995.

There was a further wage slowdown in the early 2000s, which was probably linked to the 'China shock' (see Chapter 4) and after 2007, when the financial crisis took hold. But then real wages started to rise again after 2015, even as China's share of global trade continued to grow. There are many potential explanations for the long-term real wage slow-down, but trade is not the likeliest culprit. As Noah Smith explains, the share of imports in US GDP was flat during the wage stagnation period before 1995, but was increasing after 1995, when real wages rose again.[25]

More and more debt

Leaving aside their effects on inequality, the budget proposals of President Trump and the Republicans in Congress have other dangers, especially when combined with the tariffs. They are based on the illusion that tax cuts for the better off will raise so much revenue that they will pay for themselves. Experience negates this belief. In 2017, taxes were cut substantially during the president's first term. The budget deficit that year was $666bn or 3.5 per cent of GDP; by 2019, the deficit had increased to $984bn, or 4.6 per cent of GDP.[26] The tax cuts reduced revenues, as a proportion of GDP, rather than paying for themselves.[27] (The pandemic did not strike until 2020, so this measure is not affected by it.)

President George W. Bush also cut taxes, with the gains mostly targeted at the better off, in 2001 and 2003.[28] In 2000, when Bill Clinton was in office, the US government actually recorded a budget surplus. But over the course of Mr Bush's terms in office, the US national debt rose from $5.7tn to $10tn.[29] To be fair, the last two years of his administration reflected the start of the financial crisis (although this actually had its biggest impact on the deficit in 2009).

Nevertheless, during the first quarter of the twenty-first century, the world has faced a pandemic, the financial crisis and the Russian invasion of Ukraine. The existence of such shocks, which worsen government finances, suggest that administrations should ensure they are not running up too much in the way of debt when times are good. At the very least, they should be careful about eroding the tax base.

US national debt is now around $37tn or almost four times higher than when Mr Bush left office in 2009.[30] That is more than 120 per cent of GDP,[31] although almost a quarter of this debt is owed to another part of the government, the Federal Reserve.[32] That's because the Fed bought bonds as part of the quantitative easing (QE) programme that followed the financial crisis of 2007–9. Nevertheless, the Fed has started to offload its QE holdings which means that other investors will eventually have to buy more US government bonds to fund the nation's borrowing.

There are usually plenty of willing buyers of US government debt. But the interest rate, or yield, they demand to own the debt has been creeping up. A government debt problem can accelerate when the interest rate is higher than the growth rate of the economy. Since tariffs will slow economic growth, then tax cuts for the rich risk making the debt problem substantially worse. And that means higher interest rates throughout the US economy, both for businesses and homeowners.

Whose side are they on?

While the rhetoric of the Trump administration is that they represent the interests of the working family against the 'elite', that is not borne out by their willingness to eliminate regulations that were designed to protect consumers and individual citizens. Take for example a proposal from the Consumer Financial Protection Bureau (CFPB) to limit the ability of data brokers to sell sensitive information about US citizens, such as their credit history and Social Security numbers. This attempt to protect customers was dropped by the acting head of the CFPB, Russell Vought, who was one of the authors of Project 2025, the radical blueprint for the Trump programme.[33]

Another CFPB rule that was cut was a plan to limit overdraft fees to $5 for banks with more than $10bn in assets.[34] Indeed, the administration has been attempting to gut the CFPB, which was set up in the aftermath of the 2007–9 financial crisis as a way to monitor the banks, after their misbehaviour was perceived to be responsible for the economic meltdown. Ironically, the crisis prompted the rise of the Tea Party protest movement which morphed into political backing for Mr Trump. CFPB staff have warned that the drastic cuts will mean that the bureau will be unable to provide oversight of mortgage and fair lending laws.[35] It is an area where the Trump administration is clearly favouring Wall Street over Main Street.

The Trump administration has also rolled back environmental policies, such as reducing mercury pollution in the atmosphere, and funding the replacement of lead pipes.[36] Meanwhile, cuts at the Food and Drug Administration will reduce the agency's ability to monitor the safety of pharmaceuticals and food.[37,38]

There is a big disconnect here. The cuts at the CFPB and FDA are being made in the name of deregulation – that businesses will prosper if the government does not get in their way. To restate the point, this argument is entirely counter to the thrust of tariffs, which represent the government interfering with businesses' decisions over their choice and location of suppliers. This policy incoherence leads to the theme of the final chapter: that the Trump administration has no clear plan.

6

THE MAN WITHOUT A PLAN

'They were careless people, Tom and Daisy – they
smashed up things and creatures and then retreated
back into their money or their vast carelessness, or
whatever it was that kept them together, and let other
people clean up the mess they had made.'

F. Scott Fitzgerald, *The Great Gatsby*

Analysing Donald Trump's economic policy is rather like
nailing jelly to the wall. There have been so many bewildering changes of direction, even in the course of writing this
book. We know that Mr Trump likes the principle of tariffs
but he is willing to change his mind over which countries
and which products the tariffs will apply to and at what rate
they will be levied.

After the mid-May retreat over Chinese tariff rates, investors clearly breathed a sigh of relief. Because the ridiculous
145 per cent rate had been dropped, they thought the president had seen sense. But this is a mistake. The effective tariff
rate had still risen by more than 15 percentage points to its

highest level since the 1930s.[1] Even if one court ruled against the tariff plan, Mr Trump is unlikely to give up easily and the potential for further chaos remains. While the tariffs are very bad, Mr Trump's unpredictability is even worse. A man who changed his mind yesterday may change it back tomorrow.

What is clear is that Mr Trump does not like the multi-national order that emerged after the Second World War. That regime was in part created by the great economist John Maynard Keynes, who inspired the title of this book. One of the bodies established after the war was the International Monetary Fund, which was to play an important role as the global lender of last resort over the subsequent eighty years. So, it was fitting that, in mid-April 2025, the IMF lowered its global growth estimates and declared that 'The global economic system under which most countries have operated for the last 80 years is being reset, ushering the world into a new era.' But the IMF drily added that 'Existing rules are challenged while new ones are yet to emerge.'[2]

The trading system that emerged after 1945 was developed first by the General Agreement on Tariffs and Trade (GATT) and then by the World Trade Organization (WTO). The guiding principle was to create a climate where, as much as possible, nations treated each other equally. The result, over the decades, was a substantial decline in tariffs and an enormous expansion in global trade.

The Trump administration is determined to smash this trading system but it is far from clear what it would like to see in its place. The strongest impression one gets is that the 'smashing' is the main point. Such turmoil resembles the 'continuous revolution' strategy of Mao Zedong rather than the sensible stewardship of a developed economy.

As Joey Politano, an economic analyst, exclaimed in frustration: 'The administration has never put out a single chart about tariffs. They've never put out a single paper on the policy goals of the tariffs. They've never put out even the things that they're supposed to. They're supposed to put out a revenue estimate for tax purposes. They've never put one out. And so it's really hard to judge what they're actually trying to achieve.'[3]

The best guess is that Mr Trump does not like a multi-lateral system because it constrains his actions (indeed, he does not like any other institution constraining his actions). He would much rather deal bilaterally with other nations, since this increases his leverage (and he might get use of the occasional plane[4]). But such an approach makes trade much less predictable and is likely to constrain business invest-ment and economic growth.

Very careless people

The quote which starts this chapter is taken from *The Great Gatsby*, published on 10 April 1925, almost exactly 100 years to the day before the Trump tariff package was unveiled. Like Tom and Daisy, Trump and the many billionaires in his coterie can cause vast destruction to the economy and then retreat back into their privileged lives. They will always be fine. It will be for others – politicians in later administrations, leaders of other countries, business executives and, most importantly, the citizens of the US and elsewhere – to clear up the mess.

About some things, the Trump administration had

a strong case to make. China does treat foreign nations unfairly when it comes to trade, and Chinese citizens would undoubtedly benefit if it switched from an export-based model to one where domestic consumption was encouraged. So too would the world; Chinese consumer spending might be a powerful engine for global growth. Mr Trump is also correct when he says that European nations have spent too little on their own defence and have been too reliant on the US for security. And his popularity stems in part from a genuine grievance: ordinary workers in the US have experienced a long period of sluggish real wage growth.

But Mr Trump's approach to solving these problems is counterproductive, destroying when he could have been building. On the issue of China, there might have been an opportunity to find common cause with other countries that feel they get a raw deal from the Chinese government. That was the approach taken by President Obama, who patiently negotiated a Trans-Pacific Partnership (TPP) which included twelve nations, such as Canada, Mexico, Australia, New Zealand, and important Asian countries such as Japan, Singapore and Vietnam, but not China. The Brookings Institution concluded that the agreement 'would have contributed positively to US economic growth, and could have also enhanced American influence in Asia and in the world by reassuring allies and rivals that the United States is a multi-dimensional resident power'.[5]

But Mr Trump withdrew the US from the TPP on the first day of his first term in office. The remaining eleven powers forged ahead with the agreement, and the UK joined in 2024. In the aftermath of the 2 April tariff announcement, there was talk of the alliance, now renamed CPTPP (the extra letters stand for 'comprehensive' and 'progressive'), being used as a free-trade hub for those countries hardest hit by the levies. So, in an ironic twist, an agreement originally devised to isolate China may turn into one that isolates the US instead.

The Trump administration also seems to have significantly underestimated the strength of China's negotiating position. 'They're playing with a pair of twos,' Scott Bessent said of the Chinese. 'What do we lose by the Chinese raising tariffs on us? We export one-fifth to them of what they export to us, so that is a losing hand for them.'[6]

Again, this misunderstands the nature of trade. Countries import goods and services because they want those products. If they don't trade, they don't get the merchandise. 'The United States gets vital goods from China that cannot be replaced any time soon or made at home at anything less than prohibitive cost,' wrote Adam Posen of the Peterson Institute.[7] He added 'given that the US economy is entirely dependent on Chinese sources for vital goods (pharmaceutical stocks, cheap electronic chips, critical minerals), it is wildly reckless not to ensure alternate suppliers or adequate domestic production *before* cutting off trade.'

An experienced China watcher might also have realised that President Xi would react badly to being bullied. This instinct is partly inspired by the 'century of national humiliation' after 1842 when parts of China were occupied by foreign powers. In 2025, the Chinese economy is strong enough to bear a bit of financial pain; better that than losing face in a foreign-policy dispute.

When Mr Trump dropped the 145 per cent tariff rates on China in May, he did not win any significant concessions from Beijing. The Chinese simply removed the retaliatory levies they had imposed. Having called Mr Trump's bluff once, the Chinese may be inclined to call it again.

Alienating the allies

As for Europe, Mr Trump's actions certainly prompted many EU nations to announce plans to increase their defence spending. But his hostile approach to old allies came at considerable cost to the US's 'soft power': its ability to influence other nations. Friedrich Merz, the chancellor of Germany, who had previously been a strong supporter of an alliance with the US, had a Damascene conversion. In February 2025 he said, 'My absolute priority will be to strengthen Europe as quickly as possible so that, step by step, we can really achieve independence from the USA.' He added that 'After Donald Trump's statements last week, it is clear that the Americans, at least this part of the Americans, this administration, are largely indifferent to the fate of Europe.'[8]

Europe's reactions were driven not just by Mr Trump's demands on defence spending, but also by his apparent hostility to the cause of Ukraine, which has been battling a Russian invasion since 2022. While the Biden administration had seen supporting Ukraine as an essential element in supporting democracy against Russian autocracy, Mr Trump thought this was a sucker's bet. Instead, his main interest in Ukraine seemed to involve a deal to secure the country's mineral wealth. He felt that Russian territorial gains should be officially recognised.

Asked if he could rule out the use of military force to seize both Greenland and the Panama Canal, he said, 'No, I can't assure you either of those two,' before adding that 'We need Greenland for national security purposes.'[9] This was a big shock for European countries who had relied on the NATO alliance since 1949 for security against Russian aggression. It undermined the idea of the US as a benign superpower that would act in a fundamentally different way from Russia or China.

For example, allies would not normally expect the US to campaign against their existing government. But Mr Trump has repeatedly dubbed Canada 'the 51st state' and called for its absorption into the US, while mocking former prime minister Justin Trudeau as 'Governor' Trudeau. The result was a dramatic turnaround in the polls as Trudeau's replacement as Liberal leader, Mark Carney, won an election in April 2025 because of his perceived ability to stand up to Mr Trump while his Conservative opponent lost his seat. Shortly afterwards, Anthony Albanese, the Australian prime minister, won an easy re-election because his opponent was deemed to resemble Mr Trump. This is a new phenomenon in the democratic world – election results being driven by public opposition to a US president.

Soft power, hard cash

Why does all this matter to the US economy? Soft power has widespread effects. It makes the US an appealing place to live and work and makes the goods and services it produces more attractive. When soft power dissipates, the effects can also be widespread. European car buyers turned against the

Tesla brand of electric cars, a company run by Elon Musk, whose controversial statements included an intervention in the German election backing the far-right AfD party. This was a spectacular misjudgement on Mr Musk's part since the consumers most willing to buy electric cars are likely to be more concerned about climate change, and more liberal in politics.

In March 2025, Tesla's European sales were down 49 per cent year on year even as overall electric vehicle sales were up 28 per cent.[10] The automobile sector is one of the industries Mr Trump most wants to help, and Tesla is the US's most valuable car group in stock-market terms. The president was reduced to having a Tesla car show at the White House in a bid to boost sales.

Another economic impact emerged in the tourism sector. In March 2025, there were sharp drops in the number of people flying to the US from the UK (down 15 per cent from March 2024), Spain (25 per cent), Ireland (27 per cent) and Germany (29 per cent).[11] The effect was even greater in Canada, whose very existence was threatened by Trump's rhetoric; at one point in March, bookings on Canadian flights to the US were down 70 per cent year on year.[12]

A decline in tourism does have an economic impact. Indeed, it is worth noting that inbound tourism counts as an export (it brings in revenues from abroad). For a country attempting to reduce its balance of payments deficit, discouraging tourism is pushing the numbers in the wrong direction.

Foreigners have also been concerned about a crackdown on immigration that has caught some tourists in its net.[13]

One Welsh tourist was shackled and detained for nineteen days when trying to leave the country;[14] a French academic was reportedly denied entry after border officials found messages critical of Trump's policies on his personal devices.[15] Whatever the exact details of the stories, they created the perception of an extra risk for anyone thinking of visiting the US.

That concern will only have been heightened by the deportation of alleged Venezuelan gang members to El Salvador without trial, and in defiance of court orders to allow them to stay.[16] A sense that justice is arbitrary and cruel in the US weakens the image of the country as the 'land of the free' and a beacon of democracy. The Democracy Perception Index, a survey of public opinion across the world, found that the proportion of countries where the public had a positive perception of the US had dropped from 76 per cent in 2024 to 45 per cent in April 2025.[17]

Tell me what you want, what you really really want

A lot has been made of Mr Trump's prowess as a deal-maker. But the Trump decision-making process is so chaotic that other countries do not know how to negotiate with the US. 'What does this administration exactly want? Do they want a new trade deal? Do they want tariffs? We just don't know,' Eelco Heinen, the Dutch finance minister, told the *Financial Times* in April.[18]

Japan was one of the first countries to attempt to enter trade negotiations with the US and President Trump quickly announced that the talks were making good progress. But reporters who talked to the Japanese heard the complaint that the US kept changing its demands. Chas Freeman, a former US ambassador, recounted that 'the American leadership said, "What are you offering?" And the Japanese said, "Well, what is it that you want?" And the Americans could not explain what they wanted.'[19]

One report noted Japanese frustration that the Americans were citing a supposed 700 per cent tariff on rice and, for automotives, a 'bowling ball test', involving dropping a ball onto the hood of a car from 20 feet to see if it would dent it. Neither provision exists.[20] Such misunderstandings make it very difficult to see how negotiations with Japan can end before the ninety-day hiatus on heightened tariffs expires. In turn, that explains why the Trump administration gave up on negotiating with most countries and announced it would set tariff rates unilaterally.

Other nations are unlikely to see Mr Trump as a reliable negotiating partner. In 2018, the US, Mexico and Canada entered into a new trade agreement (called the USMCA for obvious reasons) that replaced the North American Free Trade Agreement (NAFTA) that Mr Trump had frequently denounced. The president described the pact his administration negotiated as 'a great deal for all three countries' that 'greatly opens markets to our farmers and manufacturers'.[21] But when he returned to office in 2025, Canada and Mexico were among the first countries that Mr Trump hit with tariffs. The logical conclusion is that offering a deal to Mr Trump is like paying a blackmailer: he will always be back for more.

The UK has generally been a loyal ally of the US, backing it in its invasions of Afghanistan and Iraq, for example. Sir

Keir Starmer, the prime minister, laid the flattery on thick with Mr Trump, promising him an unprecedented second state visit to the UK in his first appointment in the Oval Office in February 2025. But Britain's initial reward, even though the US has balanced trade with the UK, was to be hit by the standard 10 per cent tariff and, initially, to be subject to extra tariffs on cars, steel and aluminium.

The UK was first to do a deal with the US, announced on 8 May. Actually, 'deal' is too strong a word. This was a framework agreement which states on the first page (of a five-page memo) that 'both the United States and the United Kingdom recognize that this document does not constitute a legally binding agreement'.[22] The tariff on UK cars was cut from 25 per cent to 10 per cent (only on the first 100,000 vehicles sold) and tariffs on Britain's tiny steel industry cut to zero. Despite this apparent concession, the 'deal' was so vague that, when Mr Trump raised steel tariffs to 50 per cent in late May, it wasn't immediately clear whether the UK was exempt. In return, Britain reduced tariffs on US beef and ethanol. The US definitely got the better end of the deal, since the average tariffs charged on US goods were lower than before Mr Trump took office while those on British goods were higher.

However the agreement did nothing for US manufacturers; unsurprisingly since the UK wasn't excluding US goods in the first place. Alan Beattie, the *Financial Times*'s trade editor, remarked tartly that 'the pact is closer to a protection payment to a mob boss than a liberalising agreement between sovereign countries'.[23] There was nothing in the package to prevent the US from demanding more concessions later.

Faith and credit

Investors have also had their faith in US policymaking severely tested. As previously noted, the US stock market, bond market and dollar all fell in the aftermath of the 2 April announcement. This was highly unusual. As Morgan Stanley observed in a research note published on 27 April, this pattern was 'more associated with emerging than developed markets'. The bank's analysts added that 'evolving market perceptions of the trajectory of the US economy and policymaking are taking the global economy and markets to unprecedented levels of uncertainty'.[24]

This uncertainty has come as a shock to investors who have a high exposure to US assets. Such has been the enthusiasm for US shares, particularly in tech companies such as Apple, Microsoft and Alphabet (Google's parent), that, in early 2025, the US stock market comprised 70 per cent of the MSCI World Index, the most commonly used benchmark for global investors. That compares with around 30 per cent in 1988 and 50 per cent in 2000.[25]

And it is not just equities where the US dominates. As already noted, the Treasury bond market is the most liquid on the planet and through complex arrangements such as repos (with a value of around $7tn[26]) underpins the system for interbank lending. The US dollar is the most important currency for international trade, debt issuance and cross-border lending, and is the biggest component of the reserves of other central banks. This dominance will not end quickly given the lack of ready alternatives but, as Morgan Stanley remarked, 'It is hard to put the genie back in the bottle once such concerns are raised.'[27]

Investors find few signs that the Trump administration understands the problem. A meeting between Stephen Miran, chair of the Council of Economic Advisers, and some leading hedge funds ended with some participants saying Mr Miran was 'incoherent' and 'out of his depth'.[28] Ken Griffin is the founder of Citadel, a hedge fund group with $65bn in assets, and one of the most respected figures on Wall Street. He told a conference in April that 'The United States was more than just a nation, it's a universal brand. Whether it's our culture, our financial strength, our military strength, America rose beyond just being a country. It was like an aspiration for most of the world, and we're eroding that brand right now.'[29]

A loss of international investor confidence will have implications for US citizens. In May 2025, the rating agency Moody's downgraded the US's credit rating from the highest AAA level. The downgrade was followed by a spike in bond yields which means higher borrowing costs for the US government. Those higher costs will then feed through into higher borrowing costs for US companies and for US homeowners through their mortgages. A weaker dollar will raise the price of imports, regardless of the level of tariffs. And if the US stock market declines in value, that affects the long-term savings on which consumers rely.

The sell-off in bonds has been made worse by the administration's budget plans to cut taxes for the better off at a time when the deficit is already substantial and federal debt is nearly 100 per cent of GDP (and that is not counting the debt held by the Federal Reserve). In a reverse Robin Hood gambit, Mr Trump is taking money from the poor (cuts to food aid, Medicare and Medicaid) to fund this handout for the rich. But the tax cuts are much bigger than the spending reductions. The Budget passed by the Republicans in Congress also contains a clause allowing the government to tax companies and investors from countries with 'punitive' tax policies, a provision that has spooked some investors.[30]

Paradoxically, a market meltdown could be the world's best hope to rein in the worst of Trump's economic folly. He retreated once in the face of market turmoil and he may do so again. But even a retreat will not be without consequences. After the China tariff climbdown in May, the Center for Strategic and International Studies concluded that the agreement did 'not undo the significant damage already inflicted by elevated costs, disrupted supply chains, heightened uncertainty, and weakened US credibility with allies. The ongoing reliance on an erratic trade policy – marked by temporary fixes, strategic inconsistency, and persistent unpredictability – continues to undermine long-term economic resilience and US global leadership, while imposing avoidable costs on consumers and businesses alike.'[31]

The effect on workers

Perhaps the most electorally appealing part of the Trump programme is the promise that it will bring back high-paying jobs to the US, particularly in the manufacturing sector. Ordinary workers hoped that this would address a long-running imbalance. While the wages of top earners grew 46 per cent in real (after-inflation) terms between 1979 and 2023, middle-earners and low-earners saw increases of just 17 per cent.[32]

But as was noted in the last chapter, many developed nations have encountered the same pressures from globalisation but do not display the same inequalities of income and wealth as the US, and their workers tend to have more rights and benefits which shelter them from the vicissitudes of the economic cycle.

In the short term, most economists have predicted that the high tariffs will slow economic growth which will mean a pick-up in unemployment or, at the very least, fewer jobs being created. At the same time high tariffs will create shortages of goods in the shops and push up prices for consumers, while benefit cuts will hit the poorest people. Greater inequality will be one of the economic consequences of Mr Trump.

The counter-argument, made by the Trump administration, is that the disruption caused by the tariffs will just be short term in nature and that, in the long run, the result will be to bring back high-paying manufacturing jobs to the US. But the decline in manufacturing jobs in the US is part of a long-term trend that has emerged across the developed world, and is caused more by automation than by trade competition.

In the long run, economic growth is driven mainly by two factors: an increase in the number of workers and an increase in the productivity of those workers. Mr Trump is cracking down on immigration, one of the main sources of new labour. The US labour force is projected to rise more slowly in the 2023–33 period (3.7 per cent) than it did in the 2013–23 period (7.5 per cent).[33] That means productivity will have to assume more of the burden of generating growth.

But Trump's plans for the economy will create headwinds for productivity growth. US manufacturing employment may have dropped but the value added per worker has soared, and is much higher than that of China. If the tariffs force the US to shift production back home, resources will have to be moved into less productive areas, bad news for overall productivity growth.

Another component of the Trump programme that does not augur well for productivity is its aggressive drive against the nation's top universities and research programmes. The attempt to bar Harvard from accepting foreign students will cripple a university ranked third best in the world,[34] and the hostile attitude towards foreign students in general undermines a source of US soft power. It also deters a cohort that is vital for the financial health of universities and which generated $50bn of exports in 2023, the seventh-biggest services sector (like inbound tourism, money spent by foreign students within the US counts as an export).[35]

And it is not just undergraduates. Universities are home to some of the greatest scientific minds of the day who are conducting vital research, which depends on public support. The federal government funds around 40 per cent of basic research in the US, according to the National Center for Science and Engineering Statistics, but this money is now under threat.[36]

One institution that has come under attack is the National Institutes of Health (NIH). Far from being a waste of public money, funding from the NIH contributed to 99 per cent of all the drugs approved between 2010 and 2019.[37] A report from United for Medical Research found that every dollar of research funded by the NIH generated another $2.56 in economic activity.[38] But scientists from both the US and elsewhere feel that the Trump administration makes them less welcome. In the first quarter of 2025, the number of foreign researchers applying to come to the US fell by a third, compared with the same period in 2024, while applications for overseas jobs by US scientists rose by a quarter.[39]

As the National Science Foundation points out, the global competitiveness of the US depends not only on a skilled workforce, but also on the research and development which 'fosters scientific and technological breakthroughs and leads to the development of new and improved processes, services, and products'.[40] In absolute terms, the US spends more on research and development, and on basic research, than any other country, but China is catching up fast. In 2024, China's spending on research and development rose by 8.7 per cent compared with an increase of just 1.7 per cent in the US.[41]

We are the world

Some will dismiss all the arguments in this book as 'globalist'. To which the obvious retort is, we all live on this globe. Many of the biggest problems we face are global, whether they are pandemics, climate change, pollution, or the need to cope with people fleeing across borders from oppressive regimes. Such problems, among many others, need an international response. Mr Trump's actions are not just bad news for Americans, they are bad news for people all over the world, whether they lose their jobs because of the uncertainty he creates, they lose access to the foreign aid he has cut, or they lose their rights in the autocratic nations he defends.

The global nature of the economy is woven into every feature of our lives whether we drink coffee grown in Colombia, eat meat from Brazil, wear sweaters made from the wool of Australian sheep, drive cars with fuel drilled in Saudi Arabia, or watch a South Korean drama on a smartphone designed in the US but reliant on metals mined in Chile and assembled in China. This system has steadily grown over decades; overturning it will be immensely disruptive and costly. The worst effects of Mr Trump's policies are yet to be felt because businesses have brought forward activity in advance of the tariffs. But as analysts at Citibank wrote in late May, this could be 'the calm before the storm'.[42]

Perhaps the whole sorry saga of Mr Trump's misguided policies is best illustrated by the letter from the US Chamber of Commerce, the lobby group for small business, recounted in Chapter 1. The letter opens by saying its members 'appreciate your efforts to negotiate bilateral agreements with other nations'. Having got the flattery over, it then mentions that small businesses 'are seeing their ability to survive endangered' before asking for the exclusion from the tariffs of small businesses in general, goods that cannot be produced in the US in particular and any tariffs that might endanger US jobs.[43]

The complaint brings to mind the film *Monty Python's Life of Brian* where Reg (John Cleese) forcefully dismisses the benefits of Roman rule. After a series of factual interjections from his comrades, he concludes defiantly 'apart from the sanitation, the medicine, education, wine, public order, irrigation, roads, a fresh water system, and public health, what have the Romans ever done for us?'

One could sum up the message of this book, in the style of Monty Python, by saying, 'Apart from the failed businesses, lost jobs, goods shortages, hits to consumer and business confidence, weakening of the relationship with key allies and decline of the US's international reputation, Trump has a brilliant plan.'

Few people have expertise in a wide range of areas. And few people will govern wisely if they lack advisers who are willing to challenge their views. The excruciating sight of Cabinet members competing to shower Mr Trump with praise is reminiscent of some tinpot dictatorship, not the world's most powerful democracy. It is no wonder policymaking is so chaotic. Some Americans yearn for strong leadership but all they have got is the wrong leadership.

The Dunning–Kruger effect describes the tendency for people with low competence in a particular field to overestimate their abilities. Mr Trump has no expertise in international trade, and refuses to listen to people who do. He made up his mind about trade in the 1980s and since he thinks he can never be wrong, he is not going to change now. He is smashing a system he does not understand, and he does not know how to replace it. Even if he now abandons his policy altogether, or the courts block it permanently, the moment when he unveiled nonsensical tariff rates on 2 April will serve as a lesson for future politicians on what *not* to do.

And if he does not change course significantly, the whole world will suffer the adverse economic consequences of Mr Trump.

NOTES

Introduction

1 Inga Fechner and Rico Luman, 'Importing European cars into the US? Prepare for a price shock', ING, 28 March 2025, think.ing.com/articles/importing-european-cars-into-the-us-prepare-for-a-price-shock

2 'Trump tells Walmart to "eat the tariffs" instead of raising prices', *City AM*, 17 May 2025, cityam.com/trump-tells-walmart-to-eat-the-tariffs-instead-of-raising-prices/

3 John Maynard Keynes, *The Economic Consequences of the Peace* (London: Macmillan and Co., 1919)

4 samsung.com/us/aboutsamsung/sustainability/supply-chain/supplier-list/

5 'Why Trump can't build iPhones in the US', *Financial Times*, 28 April 2025, ig.ft.com/us-iphone/

6 *Poverty, Prosperity, and Planet Report 2024: Pathways out of the Polycrisis* (Washington, DC: World Bank, 2024), worldbank.org/en/publication/poverty-prosperity-and-planet

7 Saloni Dattani et al., 'Life expectancy', Our World in Data (2023), ourworldindata.org/life-expectancy

8 x.com/MikeDrucker/status/1917640525915591090

9 fdra.org/wp-content/uploads/2025/04/April-29-Footwear-POTUS-Letter.pdf

10 Dorothy Neufeld, 'Mapped: average tariff rates by country', Visual Capitalist, 3 April 2025, visualcapitalist.com/tariff-rates-by-country

11 Davide Furceri et al., 'Are tariffs bad for growth? Yes, say five decades

of data from 150 countries', *Journal of Policy Modeling* 42:4 (2020), pp. 850–9, doi.org/10.1016/j.jpolmod.2020.03.009

12 Ian Smith et al., 'US borrowing costs climb after Moody's downgrade', *Financial Times*, 19 May 2025, ft.com/content/c1f34949-86fc-4e70-90c9-4e2e49ed2a29

13 assets.publishing.service.gov.uk/media/681d327d43d6699b3c1d2a9d/US_UK_EPD_050825_FINAL_rev_v2.pdf

14 Timothy Garton Ash, 'Brace for disorder as the great power shifts begin', *Financial Times*, 9 May 2025, ft.com/content/e45091ae-31c7-46b2-95bb-b8197655cd33

1. Where there is order, let there be chaos

1 Antoine Gara et al., 'How Wall Street got Donald Trump wrong', *Financial Times*, 14 April 2025, ft.com/content/e0b28b01-3cdb-4c64-be28-93f51b4a21e6

2 Kevin Corinth and Stan Veuger, 'President Trump's tariff formula makes no economic sense. It's also based on an error', American Enterprise Institute, 4 April 2025, aei.org/economics/president-trumps-tariff-formula-makes-no-economic-sense-its-also-based-on-an-error/

3 Josie Ensor, 'Trump used my research to calculate tariffs – but got it wrong', *The Times*, 8 April 2025

4 Corinth and Veuger, op. cit.

5 Peter Fabricius, 'Could Africa still be hard hit by Trump's tariff tantrum?', Institute for Security Studies, 11 April 2025, issafrica.org/iss-today/could-africa-still-be-hard-hit-by-trump-s-tariff-tantrum

6 James Politi, 'India and Brazil to be hit hardest under US reciprocal tariffs, says Capital Economics', *Financial Times*, 13 February 2025, ft.com/content/bcc61d3b-bdc6-4f19-be1b-944e0be213c1#post-ofae69fe-8b74-456d-a1b9-f04358399846

7 Ben Blatt, Francesca Paris and Ethan Singer, 'The hidden decisions behind Trump's tariff formula', *The New York Times*, 4 April 2025, nytimes.com/interactive/2025/04/04/upshot/trump-tariffs-reciprocal.html

8 Ottilie Mitchell, 'US defends tariffs on remote island of penguins and seals', BBC News, 7 April 2025, bbc.co.uk/news/articles/ce84jr5mvnn0

9 Gabe Whisnant and Sonam Sheth, 'Donald Trump personally decided

his new tariff rates: report', *Newsweek*, 4 April 2025, newsweek.com/donald-trump-personally-decided-his-new-tariff-rates-report-2055571

10 Paul Krugman, 'Will malignant stupidity kill the world economy?', Substack post, 3 April 2025, paulkrugman.substack.com/p/will-careless-stupidity-kill-the

11 Corinth and Veuger, op. cit.

12 David Smith, 'Trump says "I know what I'm doing" before stepping back from global tariffs', *Guardian*, 9 April 2025, theguardian.com/us-news/2025/apr/09/trump-address-republicans-china-tariffs

13 Alison Durkee, 'Will Trump negotiate tariffs? JD Vance says president wants to "rebalance global trade" – but no deals reached yet', *Forbes*, 22 April 2025, forbes.com/sites/alisondurkee/2025/04/22/will-trump-negotiate-tariffs-jd-vance-says-president-wants-to-rebalance-global-trade-but-no-deals-reached-yet/

14 Cecelia Smith-Schoenwalder, 'Fact-checking Trump's fentanyl justification for tariffs on Canada, Mexico and China', *U.S. News & World Report*, 4 April 2025, usnews.com/news/national-news/articles/2025-04-04/how-much-fentanyl-is-coming-from-canada-mexico-and-china-fact-checking-trumps-tariff-justification

15 Kate Dore, 'Trump said "there is a chance" tariff revenue could replace the income tax. Economists are skeptical', CNBC, 22 April 2025, cnbc.com/2025/04/22/trump-tariffs-replace-income-tax.html

16 Caroline Valetkevitch, 'S&P 500 loses $5 trillion in two days in Trump tariff selloff', Reuters, 5 April 2025, reuters.com/markets/global-markets-wrapup-1-2025-04-04/

17 Kevin Breuninger, 'Trump blames "globalists" for stock market sell-off', CNBC, 6 March 2025, cnbc.com/2025/03/06/trump-blames-globalists-for-stock-market-sell-off.html

18 Rachel Barenblat, 'Is ranting against globalism antisemitic?', Forward, 24 October 2018, forward.com/community/412627/globalism-anti-semitism/

19 fiscaldata.treasury.gov/interest-expense-avg-interest-rates/

20 fred.stlouisfed.org/series/DGS30

21 Arjun Neil Alim et al., 'US Treasuries sell-off deepens as "safe haven" status challenged', *Financial Times*, 9 April 2025, ft.com/content/0005e091-930d-46ff-9e81-8591704a9282

22 Alexander Saeedy and Josh Dawsey, 'Trump advisers took advantage of

Navarro's absence to push for tariff pause', *Wall Street Journal*, 18 April 2025, wsj.com/politics/policy/trump-tariff-pause-navarro-bessent-lutnick-b9e864fb

23 Robert Armstrong, 'Taco trade theory and the US market's surprise comeback', *Financial Times*, 1 May 2025, ft.com/content/e81ae481-fbb6-47e7-bd6b-c7d76ca5ab69

24 Brett Samuels, 'Trump responds to TACO trade criticisms: "You call that chickening out?"', *The Hill*, 28 May 2025, thehill.com/business/5321877-trump-defends-trade-strategy-taco/

25 'Empire State manufacturing survey', April 2025, newyorkfed.org/survey/empire/empiresurvey_overview

26 Ibid.

27 Robert Schoenberger, 'Manufacturing business confidence plummets in April', *IndustryWeek*, 17 April 2025, industryweek.com/the-economy/news/55283901/manufacturing-business-confidence-plummets-in-april

28 Alex Irwin-Hunt, 'A trade crunch is coming for US ports', *fDi Intelligence*, 7 May 2025, fdiintelligence.com/content/a890d306-5fec-4e44-9e3b-5b2e57622a0c

29 Sam Fleming and Claire Jones, 'How the US trade war is infecting the global economy', *Financial Times*, 25 April 2025, ft.com/content/14c336eb-e20a-40ae-a97f-644859oc0c49

30 Peter Foster et al., 'Demand slump fuelled by Trump tariffs hits US ports and air freight', *Financial Times*, 27 April 2025, ft.com/content/967a0c1a-6ae5-4d72-bd78-b7a8bdabccea

31 Terry Lane, 'Shipping rates rise as exports from China surge', Investopedia, 21 May 2025, investopedia.com/shipping-rates-rising-as-volumes-from-china-surge-on-tariffs-pause-11739120

32 'Don't blame imports for the fall in America's GDP', *Economist*, 1 May 2025, economist.com/finance-and-economics/2025/05/01/dont-blame-imports-for-the-fall-in-americas-gdp

33 Fin Daniel Gómez and Richard Escobedo, 'Walmart, Target CEOs privately warned Trump tariffs could lead to empty shelves soon', CBS News, 23 April 2025, cbsnews.com/news/walmart-target-trump-tariff-supply-chains

34 'How Donald Trump might steal Christmas', *Economist*, 24 April 2025,

economist.com/business/2025/04/24/how-donald-trump-might-steal-christmas

35 Kana Inagaki and Claire Bushey, 'GM pauses share buybacks over Trump tariff uncertainty', *Financial Times*, 29 April 2025, ft.com/content/c7d93978-9048-4f72-b049-7b19124fcd94

36 Kana Inagaki, 'General Motors to deploy "Covid playbook" to offset $5bn tariff hit', *Financial Times*, 1 May 2025, ft.com/content/5b8e9e5b-8f85-4f72-8fc4-3f93e03f09ae

37 Claire Bushey, 'Ford expects $1.5bn profit hit from Trump tariffs', *Financial Times*, 5 May 2025, ft.com/content/c0561a20-137b-49be-8eb4-d5aaaa8e5763

38 uschamber.com/assets/documents/Administration-Letter-on-Tariffs.pdf

39 conference-board.org/topics/consumer-confidence

40 Wells Fargo Research Team, 'Consumer confidence: not optimistic, but less pessimistic', FXStreet, 27 May 2025, fxstreet.com/analysis/consumer-confidence-not-optimistic-but-less-pessimistic-202505271547

41 'Press briefing transcript: World Economic Outlook, spring meetings 2025', IMF, 22 April 2025, imf.org/en/News/Articles/2025/04/22/tr-04222025-weo-press-briefing

2. Trade is the essence of modern life

1 'Scientists discover evidence of early human innovation, pushing back evolutionary timeline', Smithsonian Institute, 15 March 2018, si.edu/newsdesk/releases/scientists-discover-evidence-early-human-innovation-pushing-back-evolutionary-timeline

2 Christopher Edens, 'Dynamics of trade in the ancient Mesopotamian "world system"', *American Anthropologist* 92:1 (March 1992), knowledgebasedsociety.com/wp-content/uploads/2021/12/680040.pdf

3 featured.undp.org/multidimensional-poverty

4 'Evolution of trade under the WTO: handy statistics', WTO, wto.org/english/res_e/statis_e/trade_evolution_e/evolution_trade_wto_e.htm

5 Douglas Irwin, 'Does trade reform promote economic growth? A review of recent evidence', World Bank Research Observer (2024), sites.dartmouth.edu/dirwin/files/2024/06/Irwin-WBRO-2024.pdf

6 'The contentious U.S.–China trade relationship', Council on Foreign

Relations, 14 April 2025, cfr.org/backgrounder/contentious-us-china-trade-relationship

7   Joe Leahy et al., 'How China's record trade surplus helped spark Trump's tariff war', *Financial Times*, 9 April 2025, ig.ft.com/china-trade-surplus/

8   Kwan S. Kim, 'The Korean Miracle (1962–1980) revisited: myths and realities in strategy and development', Kellogg Institute (November 1991), doi.org/10.7274/26126665.v1

9   Ana Maria Santacreu and Heting Zhu, 'How did South Korea's economy develop so quickly?', Federal Reserve Bank of St Louis blog, 20 March 2018, stlouisfed.org/on-the-economy/2018/march/how-south-korea-economy-develop-quickly

10   worldbank.org/en/country/vietnam/overview

11   'The dynamics of FDI into the US', private research note, 22 May 2025

12   'The federal budget in fiscal year 2024: an infographic', Congressional Budget Office, 20 March 2025, cbo.gov/publication/61181

13   budgetmodel.wharton.upenn.edu/issues/2025/5/19/house-reconciliation-bill-budget-economic-and-distributional-effects-may-19-2025

14   Martin Wolf, 'The old global economic order is dead', *Financial Times*, 6 May 2025, ft.com/content/49e38ee8-f37e-47da-8ee4-1631175d2224

15   Ana Swanson, '"Totally silly." Trump's focus on trade deficit bewilders economists', *The New York Times*, 9 April 2025, nytimes.com/2025/04/09/business/economy/trump-trade-deficit-tariffs-economist-doubts.html

3. A tax on efficiency

1   Philip Coggan, 'A world of robber barons', *Economist*, 20 February 2014, economist.com/special-report/2014/02/20/a-world-of-robber-barons

2   William Bernstein, *A Splendid Exchange: How Trade Shaped the World* (London: Atlantic Books, 2008)

3   Ibid.

4   Kris James Mitchener, Kirsten Wandschneider and Kevin Hjortshøj O'Rourke, 'The Smoot–Hawley trade war', Cato Institute, 3 November 2021, cato.org/research-briefs-economic-policy/smoot-hawley-trade-war

5   Bernstein, op. cit.

6   Chad P. Bown and Douglas A. Irwin, 'The GATT's starting point: tariff levels circa 1947', National Bureau of Economic Research, Working Paper 21782 (December 2015), doi.org/10.3386/w21782

7   Monia Snoussi-Mimouni and Edvinas Drevinskas, 'Tariffs applied by WTO members have almost halved since 1996', 13 April 2023, wto.org/english/blogs_e/data_blog_e/blog_dta_13apr23_e.htm

8   Jim Tankersley and Mark Landler, 'Trump's love for tariffs began in Japan's '80s boom', *The New York Times*, 15 May 2019, nytimes.com/2019/05/15/us/politics/china-trade-donald-trump.html

9   Alonso de Gortari, 'Reassessing value-added cross-border supply chains', Federal Reserve Bank of Dallas, dallasfed.org/research/pubs/usmca/degortari

10 Galina Hale et al., 'How much do we spend on imports?', Federal Reserve Bank of San Francisco, 7 January 2019, frbsf.org/research-and-insights/publications/economic-letter/2019/01/how-much-do-we-spend-on-imports/

11 fdra.org/wp-content/uploads/2025/04/April-29-Footwear-POTUS-Letter.pdf

12 'What an Iowa farmer fears about the trade war', 'The Daily' podcast, *The New York Times*, 24 April 2025, nytimes.com/2025/04/24/podcasts/the-daily/iowa-farmer-trade-war.html

13 Lauren Aratani and David Smith, 'Trump announces sweeping new tariffs, upending decades of US trade policy', *Guardian*, 2 April 2025, theguardian.com/us-news/2025/apr/02/trump-new-tariffs-liberation-day

14 'Average tariff rates, global, 1988 to 2015', Our World in Data, ourworldindata.org/grapher/average-tariff-rates-per-cent-19882016

15 Dorothy Neufeld, 'Mapped: average tariff rates by country', Visual Capitalist, 3 April 2025, visualcapitalist.com/tariff-rates-by-country

16 Sebastian Edwards, 'The U.S. current account deficit: gradual correction or abrupt adjustment?' *Journal of Policy Modeling* 28:6 (2006), pp. 629–43, doi.org/10.1016/j.jpolmod.2006.06.012

17 macrotrends.net/global-metrics/countries/wld/world/tariff-rates

18 data.worldbank.org/indicator/BN.CAB.XOKA.GD.ZS?locations=US

19 Davide Furceri et al., 'The macroeconomy after tariffs', World Bank Economic Review (2021), hdl.handle.net/10986/40906

20 Davide Furceri et al., 'Are tariffs bad for growth? Yes, say five decades

of data from 150 countries', *Journal of Policy Modeling* 42:4 (2020), pp. 850–9, doi.org/10.1016/j.jpolmod.2020.03.009

21 'State of U.S. tariffs: April 15, 2025', The Budget Lab, 15 April 2025, budgetlab.yale.edu/research/state-us-tariffs-april-15-2025

22 Benn Steil and Elisabeth Harding, 'Where will Trump's tariff revenues go? His first term provides a big clue', Council on Foreign Relations, 3 February 2025, cfr.org/blog/where-will-trumps-tariff-revenues-go-his-first-term-provides-a-big-clue

23 David Autor et al., 'Help for the heartland? The employment and electoral effects of the Trump tariffs in the United States', National Bureau of Economic Research, Working Paper 32082 (January 2024), doi.org/10.3386/w32082

24 Ed Conway, 'Tariffs have a long history in the US – two charts tell that story', Sky News, 22 January 2025, news.sky.com/story/tariffs-have-a-long-history-inIthe-us-two-charts-tell-that-story-13294364

25 fiscaldata.treasury.gov/americas-finance-guide/government-revenue/

26 'Tracking the Trump tariffs', Tax Policy Center, 12 May 2025, taxpolicycenter.org/features/tracking-trump-tariffs

27 bea.gov/news/2025/us-international-trade-goods-and-services-december-and-annual-2024

28 ustr.gov/countries-regions/china-mongolia-taiwan/peoples-republic-china

29 S. V. Date, 'Company boasts spending up to $20 million on Trump crypto coin to buy influence', MSN, 3 May 2025, msn.com/en-us/money/markets/company-boasts-spending-up-to-20-million-on-trump-crypto-coin-to-buy-influence/ar-AA1E4Y1D?ocid=finance-verthp-feeds

30 Philip Stafford and Will Schmitt, 'Donald Trump's memecoin surges as holders compete for private dinner with US president', *Financial Times*, 23 April 2025, ft.com/content/a7021fe9-9dea-4429-83ab-887913bc9b6e

31 Brian Beers, 'The Whitewater scandal: what you should know', Investopedia, 29 November 2024, investopedia.com/ask/answers/08/whitewater-scandal.asp

32 Oliver Hawkins, Eade Hemingway and Nikou Asgari, 'Donald Trump's crypto project netted $350mn from presidential memecoin', *Financial Times*, 7 March 2025, ft.com/content/cb1def8f-53a6-478e-9b3e-33c383b29629

33 constitutioncenter.org/the-constitution/articles/article-i#article-section-8

34 Samuel Estreicher and Andrew Babbitt, 'Are tariffs an emergency power?', Lawfare, 3 April 2025, lawfaremedia.org/article/are-tariffs-an-emergency-power

35 bea.gov/news/2025/gross-domestic-product-4th-quarter-and-year-2024-third-estimate-gdp-industry-and

36 Daniel Harari, 'GDP international comparisons: economic indicators', House of Commons Library, 3 June 2025, commonslibrary.parliament.uk/research-briefings/sn02784/

37 usinflationcalculator.com/inflation/current-inflation-rates

38 fred.stlouisfed.org/series/UNRATE

39 Simon Rabinovitch and Henry Curr, 'The American economy has left other rich countries in the dust', Economist, 14 October 2024, economist.com/special-report/2024/10/14/the-american-economy-has-left-other-rich-countries-in-the-dust

40 Maria Solovieva and Andrew Foran, 'The non-starter playbook of the Mar-a-Lago Accord', TD Economics, 1 May 2025, economics.td.com/us-mar-a-lago-accord

41 Sandra Sequeira, 'Corruption, trade costs, and gains from tariff liberalization: evidence from southern Africa', American Economic Review 106:10 (2016), pp. 3029–6, doi.org/10.1257/aer.20150313

42 Juan Carlos Hallak and Eduardo Levy Yeyati, 'Failed protectionism: what Latin America can teach us', Americas Quarterly, 14 April 2025, americasquarterly.org/article/failed-protectionism-what-latin-america-can-teach-us/

4. Where the jobs went

1 Felix Richter, 'Can Trump turn back the clock on U.S. manufacturing?', Statista, 16 April 2025, statista.com/chart/34316/share-of-manufacturing-jobs-in-us-employment/

2 Ibid.

3 David H. Autor, David Dorn and Gordon H. Hanson, 'The China shock: learning from labor market adjustment to large changes in trade', National Bureau of Economic Research, Working Paper 21906 (January 2016), doi.org/10.3386/w21906

4   data.worldbank.org/indicator/NE.IMP.GNFS.
    ZS?end=2023&locations=US-FR-DE-GB-KR-CN&start=1970&utm

5   Paul Krugman, 'A note on trade deficits and manufacturing', Substack
    post, 1 April 2025, paulkrugman.substack.
    com/p/a-note-on-trade-deficits-and-manufacturing

6   Dirk Pilat et al., 'The changing nature of manufacturing in OECD
    economies', OECD Science, Technology and Industry, Working Paper
    2006/9 (October 2006), doi.org/10.1787/308452426871

7   David Autor et al., 'Help for the heartland? The employment and
    electoral effects of the Trump tariffs in the United States', National
    Bureau of Economic Research, Working Paper 32082 (January 2024),
    doi.org/10.3386/w32082

8   Aaron Flaaen and Justin Pierce, 'Disentangling the effects of the 2018–
    2019 tariffs on a globally connected U.S. manufacturing sector', Finance
    and Economics Discussion Series 2019-086 (Washington, DC: Board of
    Governors of the Federal Reserve System, 2019), doi.org/10.17016/
    FEDS.2019.086

9   Tiago Cavalcanti, Pedro Molina Ogeda and Emanuel Ornelas, 'The
    US–China trade war creates jobs (elsewhere)', CESifo, Working Paper
    11839 (April 2025), ifo.de/sites/default/files/docbase/docs/cesifo1_
    wp11839.pdf

10 fred.stlouisfed.org/series/OUTMS

11 'Fast-forward – comparing a 1980s supercomputer to the modern
    smartphone', Adobe blog, 8 November 2022, blog.adobe.com/en/
    publish/2022/11/08/fast-forward-comparing-1980s-supercomputer-to-
    modern-smartphon

12 Michael J. Hicks and Srikant Devaraj, 'The myth and the reality of
    manufacturing in America', Center for Business and Economic
    Research, Ball State University (2015), nist.gov/system/files/
    documents/mep/data/MfgReality-1.pdf

13 Tej Parikh, 'Nostalgia for manufacturing will make the US poorer',
    Financial Times, 13 April 2025, ft.com/content/845917ed-41a5-449f-946f-
    70263adbaeb7

14 Ricardo Marto, 'What to know about the rise of services', *Economic
    Synopses* 6, Federal Reserve Bank of St Louis (2024), doi.org/10.20955/
    es.2024.6

15 'Did international trade really kill American manufacturing?',

Economist, 25 April 2025, economist.com/graphic-detail/2025/04/25/did-international-trade-really-kill-american-manufacturing

16 B. Joseph Pine II and James H. Gilmore, 'Welcome to the experience economy', *Harvard Business Review* (July–August 1998), hbr.org/1998/07/welcome-to-the-experience-economy

17 David Deming, Christopher Ong and Lawrence H. Summers, 'Technological disruption in the US labor market', in Melissa S. Kearney and Luke Pardue (eds), *Strengthening America's Economic Dynamism* (Washington, DC: Aspen Institute, 2024), economicstrategygroup.org/wp-content/uploads/2024/10/Deming-Ong-Summers-AESG-2024.pdf

18 Anne C. Case and Angus Deaton, 'Broken down by work and sex: how our health declines', National Bureau of Economic Research, Working Paper 9821 (July 2003), doi:org/10.3386/w9821

19 Jacob Pedersen et al., 'High physical work demands and working life expectancy in Denmark', *Occupational and Environmental Medicine* 77:8 (2020), pp. 567–82

20 Eric Weiner, 'Time warp: the GM strike, then and now', NPR, 26 September 2007, npr.org/2007/09/26/14720112/time-warp-the-gm-strike-then-and-now

21 'Victory of the auto workers', *America*, 28 November 1970, americamagazine.org/issue/100/victory-auto-workers

22 'Detroit: past and future of a shrinking city', Economy League, economyleague.org/resources/detroit-past-and-future-shrinking-city

23 Jaelyn Campbell, 'Auto jobs are surging in notoriously anti-union South – can the UAW find a foothold?', CBT News, 21 September 2023, cbtnews.com/the-anti-union-south-has-a-growing-demand-for-ev-jobs-uaw-is-concerned/

24 Paul Krugman, 'Democrats shouldn't support tariffs', Substack post, 14 April 2025, paulkrugman.substack.com/p/democrats-shouldnt-support-tariffs

25 Steven Greenhouse, 'America's labor unions are souring on Trump', *Slate*, 5 May 2025, slate.com/news-and-politics/2025/05/unions-donald-trump-2026-election-kilmar-abrego-garcia.html

26 bls.gov/news.release/pdf/union2.pdf

27 Ellen Dewitt, 'The most unionized states in America, ranked',

Newsweek, 5 September 2021, newsweek.com/most-unionized-states-america-ranked-1625958

28 bls.gov/news.release/pdf/union2.pdf

29 'Why Trump can't build iPhones in the US', *Financial Times*, 28 April 2025, ig.ft.com/us-iphone/

30 'The trouble with MAGA's manufacturing dream', *Economist*, 28 April 2025, economist.com/business/2025/04/28/the-trouble-with-magas-manufacturing-dream

31 Lauren Weber, 'Can Trump's tariff offensive deliver new American jobs?', *Wall Street Journal*, 11 April 2025, wsj.com/economy/trump-tariffs-manufacturing-jobs-impact

32 Michael Acton and John Reed, 'Apple turns to India to help ease Trump's China tariffs', *Financial Times*, 9 April 2025, ft.com/content/5c4b2bc9-f0ac-46f3-a93b-cfa6273428f9

33 Dan Milmo, 'Apple "aims to source all US iPhones from India", reducing reliance on China', *Guardian*, 25 April 2025, theguardian.com/technology/2025/apr/25/apple-source-us-iphones-india-china-trump-trade-war

34 Austan Goolsbee and Chad Syverson, 'The strange and awful path of productivity in the U.S. construction sector', National Bureau of Economic Research, Working Paper 30845 (February 2023), doi.org/10.3386/w30845

35 John Keilman, 'Why making an all-American product is so hard', *Wall Street Journal*, 28 April 2025, wsj.com/business/made-in-america-products-supply-chain-tariffs-06c83cea

36 Ibid.

37 Jason Miller, 'Labor shortages remain an ongoing concern in many parts of U.S. manufacturing', *Supply Chain Management Review*, 13 January 2025, scmr.com/article/labor-shortages-remain-an-ongoing-concern-in-many-parts-of-u.s-manufacturing

38 Tej Parikh, 'Nostalgia for manufacturing will make the US poorer', *Financial Times*, 13 April 2025, ft.com/content/845917ed-41a5-449f-946f-70263adbaeb7

39 Elior Cohen, 'Rising immigration has helped cool an overheated labor market', Federal Reserve Bank of Kansas City, 22 May 2024, kansascityfed.org/research/economic-bulletin/rising-immigration-has-helped-cool-an-overheated-labor-market/

40 fred.stlouisfed.org/series/PAYEMS

41 Michael A. Clemens, 'Skilled immigration on the chopping block? Effects of eliminating "Optional Practical Training" in the US', Peterson Institute for International Economics, 8 April 2025, piie.com/blogs/realtime-economics/2025/skilled-immigration-chopping-block-effects-eliminating-optional

42 John Coykendall et al., 'Taking charge: manufacturers support growth with active workforce strategies', Deloitte, 3 April 2024, deloitte.com/us/en/insights/industry/manufacturing/supporting-us-manufacturing-growth-amid-workforce-challenges.html

43 Ibid.

44 Parikh, op. cit.

45 'Surveys: special questions', Federal Reserve Bank of Dallas, 28 April 2025, dallasfed.org/research/surveys/tbos/2025/2504q

46 fred.stlouisfed.org/series/MANEMP

47 Ibid.

48 Alan Rappeport, 'Trump win shows political limits of Biden's industrial policy vision', The New York Times, 8 November 2024, nytimes.com/2024/11/08/us/politics/trump-biden-economy-manufacturing.html

49 'America's bet on industrial policy starts to pay off for semiconductors', Economist, 9 January 2025, economist.com/united-states/2025/01/09/americas-bet-on-industrial-policy-starts-to-pay-off-for-semiconductors

50 Coykendall et al., op. cit.

51 Paul Gerke, 'Trump's proposed budget cancels billions of dollars in infrastructure investments, environmental programs, research grants, and renewable energy projects', Factor This, 2 May 2025, renewableenergyworld.com/energy-business/policy-and-regulation/trumps-proposed-budget-cancels-billions-of-dollars-in-infrastructure-investments-environmental-programs-research-grants-and-renewable-energy-projects/

52 Hannah Ritchie, 'Solar panel prices have fallen by around 20% every time global capacity doubled', Our World in Data, 13 June 2024, ourworldindata.org/data-insights/solar-panel-prices-have-fallen-by-around-20-every-time-global-capacity-doubled

53 David Pierson and Berry Wang, 'DeepSeek is a win for China in the A.I. race. Will the party stifle it?', The New York Times, 2 February 2025,

nytimes.com/2025/02/02/world/asia/deepseek-china-ai-censorship.
html

54   Rogier Creemers and Louise Marie Hurel, 'Limits of economic
     deterrence in the US–China tech competition', RUSI, 14 March 2025,
     rusi.org/explore-our-research/publications/commentary/limits-
     economic-deterrence-us-china-tech-competition

55   Tsvetana Paraskova, 'Harold Hamm: "Drill, baby, drill" needs $80 oil',
     Oilprice.com, 17 March 2025, oilprice.com/Energy/Crude-Oil/Harold-
     Hamm-Drill-Baby-Drill-Needs-80-Oil.htm

56   'Saudi oil production cost up 11% in 2024', Zawya, 19 March 2025,
     zawya.com/en/projects/oil-and-gas/saudi-oil-production-cost-up-11-
     in-2024-bileicwc

5. Where all people are created unequal

1   Lauren Aratani and David Smith, 'Trump announces sweeping new
     tariffs, upending decades of US trade policy', *Guardian*, 2 April 2025,
     theguardian.com/us-news/2025/apr/02/trump-new-tariffs-liberation-
     day

2   Megan Brenan, 'Most Americans skeptical about benefits of tariffs',
     Gallup, 28 April 2025, news.gallup.com/poll/660002/americans-
     skeptical-benefits-tariffs.aspx

3   Melissa Repko, 'Walmart CFO says price hikes from tariffs could start
     later this month, as retailer beats on earnings', CNBC, 15 May 2025,
     cnbc.com/2025/05/15/walmart-wmt-q1-2026-earnings.html

4   Sarina Triangle, 'Walmart is raising prices. What will its competitors
     do?', Investopedia, 20 May 2025, investopedia.com/walmart-is-raising-
     prices-what-will-its-competitors-do-tariffs-margins-trump-11738732

5   'State of U.S. tariffs: May 12, 2025', The Budget Lab, 12 May 2025,
     budgetlab.yale.edu/research/state-us-tariffs-may-12-2025

6   Sam Joiner et al., 'The Chinese goods most Americans rely on, from
     microwaves to Barbies', *Financial Times*, 12 April 2025, ft.com/content/
     ec96e2ed-5dd6-4c6b-92a0-1b77bf517b36

7   'State of U.S. tariffs: May 12, 2025', op. cit.

8   Erica York and Alex Durante, 'Trump tariffs: tracking the economic
     impact of the Trump trade war', Tax Foundation, 2 June 2025,
     taxfoundation.org/research/all/federal/trump-tariffs-trade-war/

9   Amna Nawaz and Azhar Merchant, 'Utility assistance frozen after

Trump administration fires program's staff', PBS News, 24 April 2025, pbs.org/newshour/show/utility-assistance-frozen-after-trump-administration-fires-programs-staff

10 Catie Edmondson, 'Trump's budget flops with some powerful Republican lawmakers', *The New York Times*, 2 May 2025, nytimes.com/2025/05/02/us/politics/trump-budget-congress-republicans.html

11 Jessica Hall, 'The current Republican tax bill could cut $500 billion from Medicare – "This bill just gets more and more cruel"', MarketWatch, 21 May 2025, marketwatch.com/story/the-current-republican-tax-bill-could-cut-500-billion-from-medicare-this-bill-just-gets-more-and-more-cruel-0af411b1

12 'Extending provisions of the Tax Cuts and Jobs Act', Tax Policy Center, 27 March 2025, taxpolicycenter.org/tax-model-analysis/extending-provisions-tax-cuts-and-jobs-act

13 Brendan Duke, 'How House Republican agenda boosts the wealthy, does little (or worse) for low-income families', Center on Budget and Policy Priorities, 14 May 2025, cbpp.org/blog/how-house-republican-agenda-boosts-the-wealthy-does-little-or-worse-for-low-income-families

14 Nathaniel Weixel, 'CBO: GOP Medicaid plan would make 7.6 million people uninsured', *The Hill*, 13 May 2025, thehill.com/policy/healthcare/5298593-cbo-gop-medicaid-plan-would-make-7-6-million-people-uninsured

15 Emma Janssen, 'Republicans outdo themselves in food stamp cuts', *The American Prospect*, 15 May 2025, prospect.org/health/2025-05-15-republicans-outdo-themselves-food-stamp-cuts/

16 OECD, *Society at a Glance 2024: OECD Social Indicators* (Paris: OECD Publishing, 2024), doi.org/10.1787/918d8db3-en

17 Ibid.

18 Marcus Lu, 'Where unemployment benefits are the highest, in OECD countries', Visual Capitalist, 17 June 2024, visualcapitalist.com/unemployment-benefits-in-oecd-countries/

19 'Countries with paid sick leave 2025', World Population Review, worldpopulationreview.com/country-rankings/countries-with-paid-sick-leave

20 data.worldbank.org/indicator/SL.UEM.TOTL.ZS

21 'Manufacturing jobs as a share of total employment, 2023', Our World

in Data, ourworldindata.org/grapher/manufacturing-share-of-total-employment

22 'Which countries have the best, and worst, living standards?', *Economist*, 6 May 2025, economist.com/graphic-detail/2025/05/06/which-countries-have-the-best-and-worst-living-standards

23 x.com/LettieriDC/status/1920131600487944348

24 Noah Smith, 'So why *did* U.S. wages stagnate for 20 years?', Substack post, 18 May 2025, noahpinion.blog/p/so-why-did-us-wages-stagnate-for

25 Ibid.

26 fiscal.treasury.gov/reports-statements/financial-report/2019/government-financial-position-and-condition.html

27 fred.stlouisfed.org/series/FYFRGDA188S

28 Emily Horton, 'The legacy of the 2001 and 2003 "Bush" tax cuts', Center on Budget and Policy Priorities, 23 October 2017, cbpp.org/research/the-legacy-of-the-2001-and-2003-bush-tax-cuts

29 Hiranmayi Srinivasan, 'U.S. national debt by year', Investopedia, 25 May 2025, investopedia.com/us-national-debt-by-year-7499291

30 usdebtclock.org/

31 fred.stlouisfed.org/series/GFDEGDQ188S

32 'The federal government has borrowed trillions. Who owns all that debt?', Peter G. Peterson Foundation, 13 May 2025, pgpf.org/article/the-federal-government-has-borrowed-trillions-but-who-owns-all-that-debt/

33 Dell Cameron and Dhruv Mehrotra, 'CFPB quietly kills rule to shield Americans from data brokers', *Wired*, 14 May 2025, wired.com/story/cfpb-quietly-kills-rule-to-shield-americans-from-data-brokers/

34 Dan Ennis, 'Trump signs resolution to nix CFPB overdraft rule', Banking Dive, 12 May 2025, bankingdive.com/news/trump-sign-overturn-cfpb-overdraft-cap-rule-scott-hill-aba-lawsuit-5-dollars/747727

35 Stephanie Dhue, 'What dramatic cuts at the Consumer Financial Protection Bureau could mean for consumers', CNBC, 29 April 2025, nbcnewyork.com/news/business/money-report/what-dramatic-cuts-at-the-consumer-financial-protection-bureau-could-mean-for-consumers/6242600/

36 Julia Jacobo, 'Trump's policies could impact the environment long after he leaves office, some experts say', ABC News, 19 May 2025, abcnews.

go.com/US/trumps-policies-impact-environment-long-after-leaves-office/story?id=121749744

37   Richard G. Frank and Sherry Glied, 'The Trump administration's NIH and FDA cuts will negatively impact patients', Brookings, 14 May 2025, brookings.edu/articles/the-trump-administrations-nih-and-fda-cuts-will-negatively-impact-patients/

38   Alexander Tin, 'FDA making plans to end its routine food safety inspections, sources say', CBS News, 18 April 2025, cbsnews.com/news/fda-food-safety-inspections-plans/

6. The man without a plan

1   Greg Iacurci, 'After UK and China trade deals, tariff rate still highest since 1934, Yale report says', CNBC, 12 May 2025, cnbc.com/2025/05/12/after-uk-china-trade-deals-tariff-rate-still-highest-since-1934-yale.html

2   Pierre-Olivier Gourinchas, 'The global economy enters a new era', IMF blog, 22 April 2025, imf.org/en/Blogs/Articles/2025/04/22/the-global-economy-enters-a-new-era

3   Paul Krugman, 'Tariffs: now what?', Substack post, 17 May 2025, paulkrugman.substack.com/p/tariffs-now-what

4   Eric Lipton and Eric Schmitt, 'U.S. formally accepts luxury jet from Qatar for Trump', *The New York Times*, 21 May 2025, nytimes.com/2025/05/21/us/politics/qatar-plane-trump-air-force-one.html

5   Mireya Solís, 'Trump withdrawing from the Trans-Pacific Partnership', Brookings, 24 March 2017, brookings.edu/articles/trump-withdrawing-from-the-trans-pacific-partnership/

6   Hank Berrien, '"They're playing with a pair of twos": Treasury's Bessent warns China on escalating tariffs', Daily Wire, 8 April 2025, dailywire.com/news/theyre-playing-with-a-pair-of-twos-treasurys-bessent-warns-china-on-escalating-tariffs

7   Adam S. Posen, 'Trade wars are easy to lose', Foreign Affairs, 9 April 2025, foreignaffairs.com/united-states/tariffs-trade-wars-are-easy-lose

8   Tim Ross and Nette Nöstlinger, 'Germany's Merz vows "independence" from Trump's America, warning NATO may soon be dead', *Politico*, 23 February 2025, politico.eu/article/friedrich-merz-germany-election-united-states-donald-trump-nato/

9   'From Greenland to the Gulf of Mexico, Trump makes bold threats in

Mar-a-Lago news conference', Associated Press, 7 January 2025, newsroom.ap.org/editorial-photos-videos/detail?itemid=2d97618cdf41 4b89b578dd336c0144cd

10 Kelvin Chan, 'Tesla's monthly sales in Europe plunge by half, signaling backlash against Musk runs deep', Associated Press, 27 May 2025, apnews.com/article/tesla-elon-musk-europe-8501d6a8370b6a22c6bec7e 52de7d50c

11 Talyta França, Alessio Dell'Anna and Mert Can Yilmaz, 'Tourism boycott? Europe travel to US drops in wake of Trump presidency', Euronews, 22 April 2025, euronews.com/my-europe/2025/04/22/ tourism-boycott-europe-travel-to-us-drops-in-wake-of-trump-presidency

12 Marina Dunbar, 'Flight bookings between Canada and US down 70% amid Trump tariff war', *Guardian*, 27 March 2025, theguardian.com/ world/2025/mar/27/canada-us-flights-down-trump

13 Natalie Wilson, 'Is it safe to travel to the USA? Travel advice after tourists detained in visa crackdown', *Independent*, 28 April 2025, independent.co.uk/travel/news-and-advice/usa-travel-advice-visa-ice-b2737431.html

14 Jenny Kleeman, '"I was a British tourist trying to leave the US. Then I was detained, shackled and sent to an immigration detention centre"', *Guardian*, 5 April 2025, theguardian.com/us-news/2025/ apr/05/i-was-a-british-tourist-trying-to-leave-america-then-i-was-detained-shackled-and-sent-to-an-immigration-detention-centre

15 Samuel Osborne, 'Scientist "denied entry to US" after messages critical of Trump found on his phone', Sky News, 20 March 2025, news.sky. com/story/scientist-denied-entry-to-us-after-messages-critical-of-trump-found-on-his-phone-13332518

16 Peter Charalambous, 'Trump administration says it sent 4 alleged migrant gang members to El Salvador despite court order', ABC News, 24 April 2025, abcnews.go.com/US/trump-administration-4-alleged-migrant-gang-members-el/story?id=121121717

17 Guy Chazan, 'How Donald Trump has turned diplomacy into a combat sport', *Financial Times*, 22 May 2025, ft.com/content/f9f6a8f0-73b0-48d7-9472-6dcbd2fdfcd1

18 Sam Fleming and Claire Jones, 'How the US trade war is infecting the

global economy', *Financial Times*, 25 April 2025, ft.com/content/14c336eb-e20a-40ae-a97f-6448590c0c49

19 Jaron Schneider, 'Japan can't get an answer on what the US wants from a trade deal: report', PetaPixel, 21 April 2025, petapixel.com/2025/04/21/japan-cant-get-an-answer-on-what-the-us-wants-from-a-trade-deal-report

20 Kareem Rifai, 'Why Japan is worried after trade talks with Trump (and the rest of the world should be)', *The Diplomat*, 25 April 2025, thediplomat.com/2025/04/why-japan-is-worried-after-trade-talks-with-trump-and-the-rest-of-the-world-should-be/

21 'Trump heralds "wonderful new trade deal" to replace Nafta after Canada talks', *Guardian*, 1 October 2018, theguardian.com/us-news/2018/sep/30/nafta-talks-trump-canada-mexico-sunday-deadline

22 assets.publishing.service.gov.uk/media/681d327d43d6699b3c1d2a9d/US_UK_EPD_050825_FINAL_rev_v2.pdf

23 Alan Beattie, 'Britain's trade deal with Trump may not be good news for the world', *Financial Times*, 8 May 2025, ft.com/content/7e92d393-c08d-4be5-b349-403de6b70fbf

24 'The safe-haven question', privately distributed research note, 27 April 2025

25 msci.com/indexes/group/developed-markets-indexes

26 sifma.org/resources/research/statistics/us-repo-statistics/

27 'The safe-haven question', op. cit.

28 Kate Duguid et al., 'Top Trump adviser struggles to soothe investors in talks after market tumult', *Financial Times*, 29 April 2025, ft.com/content/a815323b-ae2b-4586-aec2-39dec35726fo

29 Yun Li, 'Citadel's Ken Griffin warns Trump about tarnishing the "brand" of U.S. Treasurys', CNBC, 23 April 2025, cnbc.com/2025/04/23/citadels-ken-griffin-warns-trump-about-tarnishing-the-brand-of-us-treasurys.html

30 Kate Duguid et al., 'Foreign tax provision in Trump budget bill spooks Wall Street', *Financial Times*, 29 May 2025, ft.com/content/b400009a-9a0e-4ee0-b6ed-2a25c2de0d8f

31 Philip Luck, 'Understanding the temporary de-escalation of the U.S.–China trade war', Center for Strategic and International Studies, 13 May 2025, csis.org/analysis/understanding-temporary-de-escalation-us-china-trade-war

32 Dorothy Neufeld, 'Charted: growth in U.S. real wages, by income group (1979–2023)', Visual Capitalist, 7 August 2024, visualcapitalist. com/growth-in-real-wages-over-time-by-income-group-usa-1979-2023/

33 bls.gov/emp/tables/civilian-labor-force-summary.htm

34 'World University Rankings 2025', *Times Higher Education*, timeshighereducation.com/world-university-rankings/latest/world-ranking

35 trade.gov/education-service-exports

36 'Analysis of federal funding for research and development in 2022: basic research', National Center for Science and Engineering Statistics, 15 August 2024, ncses.nsf.gov/pubs/nsf24332

37 Brooke Masters, 'Corporate America must stand up for the US innovation machine', *Financial Times*, 30 April 2025, ft.com/content/fi43805b-513c-4ade-942f-1f6ba7afo36a

38 Sy Boles, 'NIH funding delivers exponential economic returns', *Harvard Gazette*, 11 March 2025, news.harvard.edu/gazette/story/2025/03/nih-funding-delivers-exponential-economic-returns/

39 'MAGA's assault on science is an act of grievous self-harm', *Economist*, 22 May 2025, economist.com/leaders/2025/05/22/magas-assault-on-science-is-an-act-of-grievous-self-harm

40 'The state of U.S. science and engineering 2024: Discovery: U.S. and global R&D', National Science Foundation,13 March 2024, ncses.nsf.gov/pubs/nsb20243/discovery-u-s-and-global-r-d

41 'R&D spending growth slows in OECD, surges in China; government support for energy and defence R&D rises sharply', OECD, 31 March 2025, oecd.org/en/data/insights/statistical-releases/2025/03/rd-spending-growth-slows-in-oecd-surges-in-china-government-support-for-energy-and-defence-rd-rises-sharply.html

42 'The global impact of US tariffs', private research note, 27 May 2025

43 uschamber.com/assets/documents/Administration-Letter-on-Tariffs.pdf